Bruce E. Massis

The Practical Library Trainer

Pre-publication
REVIEWS,
COMMENTARIES,
EVALUATIONS . . .

"**B**ruce Massis presents a comprehensive overview of the current state of training in the library field and provides a vision of the workplace as a learning place that will support the profession through accelerating currents of change and recruitment and retention crises. This book is a guide and workbook for the library that strives for a supportive learning environment for its employees."

Cheryl Bryan, MLS
*Assistant Administrator for Consulting
and Continuing Education,
Southeastern Massachusetts
Library System,
Lakeville, MA*

"**B**ruce Massis has provided a resource for library managers and administrators interested in creating formal training programs within their organizations. This book provides justification for implementing such programs, guidance on funding and staffing training programs, and detailed information on evaluating the results. Massis offers a variety of information focused on training in libraries as well as outside the library sector, and provides statistics useful for comparing training in libraries with other organizations. The author's experience at SEFLIN allows him to speak not only about traditional classroom-based learning, but also about e-learning. The chapters on evaluating and determining the return on investment for training are particularly valuable for their practical suggestions offering support for ongoing training."

Susan Salomone, MPAff
*Independent Training Consultant
Fort Leavenworth, KS*

The Haworth Information Press®
An Imprint of The Haworth Press, Inc.
New York • London • Oxford

The Practical
Library Trainer

THE HAWORTH INFORMATION PRESS
Information and Library Science
Ruth C. Carter, Senior Editor

The Practical Library Trainer

Bruce Edward Massis, MLS, MA

The Haworth Information Press®
An Imprint of The Haworth Press, Inc.
New York • London • Oxford

Published by

The Haworth Information Press®, an imprint of The Haworth Press, Inc., 10 Alice Street, Binghamton, NY 13904-1580.

PUBLISHER'S NOTE
Due to the ever-changing nature of the Internet, Web site names and addresses, though verified to the best of the publisher's ability, should not be accepted as accurate without independent verification.

Cover design by Jennifer M. Gaska.

Library of Congress Cataloging-in-Publication Data

Massis, Bruce E.
    The practical library trainer / Bruce Edward Massis.
        p. cm.
    Includes bibliographical references and index.
    ISBN 0-7890-2267-2 (alk. paper)—ISBN 0-7890-2268-0 (pbk. : alk. paper)
    1. Library employees—In-service training. 2. Librarians—In-service training. 3. Library education (Continuing education) I. Title.
Z668.5.M37 2004
023'.8—dc22
                                                                                    2003016139

But the old man was wise
to show them before he died
that learning is a treasure.

Jacques Delors
Former European Commission President

ABOUT THE AUTHOR

Bruce E. Massis, MLS, MA, was chosen by *Library Journal* as one of 2002's "movers and shakers." He has served the library profession as a respected library manager for more than two decades and is currently Associate Director of the Southeast Florida Library Information Network. Previously, he was the founding Director of the JGB Cassette Recording Library International, Division Manager of the Brooklyn Public Library's Central Library, and Director of the Hoboken Public Library in New Jersey.

Mr. Massis has served in official positions within the International Federation of Library Associations and has been active in the American Library Association, the New York Library Association, the Long Island Library Association, the New Jersey Library Association, and the American Society for Training and Development. His professional publications include *Interlibrary Loan of Alternative Format Materials* (Haworth), *Serving Print Disabled Library Patrons,* and *Library Service for the Blind and Physically Handicapped: An International Approach.*

CONTENTS

Acknowledgments

I would like to thank my colleagues in the library community infused and enthused with the devotion to lifelong learning, especially my counterparts working in the library cooperatives, public, and academic staff development departments, who have supported library staff and acknowledged the power and potential of continuous education in the workplace.

Introduction

Today's information-rich environment holds a tempting array of resources from which to choose for the research process. The World Wide Web has surpassed the trillion-page mark. Each day, thousands of newly developed Web sites on every conceivable subject go live, for better or worse. Managing the quality of information available through electronic means has become an impossible task.

Libraries and their librarians, the guardians and purveyors of this information, have become increasingly important to the organization of this material and in directing the public to the appropriate resources. In order to keep abreast of the lightning-fast changes in the field, a program of staff training in libraries must be established and sustained. Reasonably skilled individuals can access these resources and become quite adept at unlocking the keys to the wealth of electronic information on the Web.

However, given the massive volume of information available electronically and via electronic means, the average library customer may become lost in a sea of information. The search for usable resource materials demands a properly trained and skilled but discerning eye. Herein lies the value of our continuously trained librarians, professionals cognizant of the pedigree, currency, and validity of library resources.

In determining the legitimacy of a research source, the library customer must place his or her faith in the knowledge and experience of the librarian. Libraries spend a great deal of their funding on "licensed" resources. These databases offer a wealth of information gathered and indexed by publishers specifically designed to provide the highest-quality content in their area of selection. However, even these products must be carefully screened, reviewed, and selected by librarians so that, through familiarity and use, they may be added to the reference tool kit for future customer recommendation.

Online database training and other electronic product familiarization is imperative. However, equally important in this electronic age is software training, so librarians can provide direct and knowledgeable public services to customers requiring assistance in the most popular and sometimes less popular software applications.

There are also "library-specific" issues dealt with every day by line staff in libraries, that is, those skills that require regular updating to remain relevant in today's information economy. Service skills must remain on the cutting edge, and this requires explicit training in specific areas of concern.

Such descriptions of the training required by working librarians may lead one to assume that library staff must be continuously enrolled in training to be effective. Although not exactly accurate, it is not too far from the truth. Learning in the library and the library *as* learning place must be synonymous. To provide the best customer service, the librarian's tool kit must be updated regularly, and not only in one single area of skill or knowledge. A library's investment in a strong and sustainable program of continuous staff training will be one of its most valuable investments, not only because it must serve a public whose expectations of service and knowledge of library staff is high, but also because the staff is the library's most important resource. For that reason, it is wise for libraries to value such programs as highly as they value their most treasured collections.

This book focuses on training in libraries for library staff not only because it is a serious issue encompassing everything in the library from providing quality customer service to reporting, to recruitment and retention of staff, but also to quell the notion of training as an "add-on" to existing staff duties. It will concentrate on the integration of staff training in libraries and how it must be viewed as a blended activity, rather than an intervention.

This work examines the organization and implementation of the library staff training program and suggests the means by which its success and market value may be determined. In the past, the notion of an actual return on investment for a program may have been seldom used in the library community, but neither libraries nor other nonprofit institutions can retain the luxury of nondisclosure. This book looks at that area of reporting as well.

Finally, this book is not designed to teach individuals how to become library trainers. Instead, it offers a comprehensive view of the staff training program in libraries from an administrator's perspective. Once the issues in this area are understood and programs implemented, the staff training program in the library can serve many functions, not the least of which can be the recruitment of needed library staff and retention of staff loyal to the institution.

Chapter 1

Preparing the Library for a Staff Training Program

As early as 1957,

> Nobel laureate Robert Solow published his theory [that] surprised many, and still surprises many today: investment in machinery cannot be a source of growth in the long run. Solow argued that the only possible source of growth in the long run is technological change.[1]

In libraries, recurrent technological change has fueled the active environment of the working librarian. In order to properly manage the growth in library usage that has coincided with this climate of change, growth must occur as an enhancement to the learning curve so that the librarian can properly manage the results of this change. Increased use of library services results from this climate of change. With such an increase comes greater workloads for library staff and any enhanced skill sets need to be developed and sharpened. There must be a convergence of librarians' knowledge and public expectation of that knowledge through a well-designed and robust library staff education and training program.

According to *USA Today,* in 2002,

> more than $686 million was spent to build 80 new libraries and renovate 132 others, a 15 percent rise in spending over a decade ago. That's the most since the $732 million spent in 1996, when the figure was skewed by the inclusion of $100 million spent on one renovation in New York City and $165

million spent in San Francisco on a new main branch. Library visits have been up 8.3 percent since March 2001, when the recession officially started. . . . [Libraries have experienced] near-record levels of spending on library construction and surges in visitors amid the economic downturn.[2]

With change a constant in libraries, a plan must be developed for sustainability of continuous education and training for librarians and library staff so that their learning curve does not level off. Employees must be encouraged to stay, and short of offering frequent raises and upgrades, other tactics must be used by management to retain staff. One of those tactics is continuous training and learning. Learning must be supported in libraries as strongly as it is supported in the private sector so that staff remain ahead of the curve rather than behind it.

Staff training in libraries has been perceived as an extravagance or, at the very least, an advantage available only to the professional staff. However, as libraries seriously consider training as a key element in the recruitment, hiring, and retention of staff *at every job level,* the importance of establishing and maintaining a continuous, comprehensive, and rigorous staff training program as a significant benefit becomes vital. Constant staff turnover can become a tremendous expense to the library. According to Frank Ofsanko and Nancy Napier,

> When an employee leaves an organization, it usually experiences substantial costs. As a result, organizations are concerned about monitoring turnover, determining the variables that influence it, and managing turnover behavior. Knowing the extent and cost of employee turnover is important to securing funds, resources, and organizational commitment which reduce turnover. The first step in measuring turnover is to define it generally as a permanent movement out of the organization. Statistically, it is usually computed as the number of employee separations divided by the total number in the workforce and expressed as a percentage.[3]

Public expectations of library staff have increased immeasurably, and it remains the responsibility of the library to measure up to these expectations. A program of continuous training in technology and in issues such as customer service, stress management, and cooperation with internal customers must also be offered to support the staff.

TYPES OF STAFF TRAINING

Types of staff training vary, and the library may offer a single example or a number of the following examples, as circumstances warrant.

1. *Formal training:* This training is planned in advance; has a structured format (time and content); has a fixed curriculum; and is conducted by a professional trainer or library employee. An example of formal training might include structured technology training through instructor-led or online delivery methods.
2. *Informal training:* This training involves on-the-job instruction, neither structured nor planned; is easily adaptable to situations, departments, or individuals; and is conducted as either one-on-one or group instruction. An example of informal training might include an employee instructing a co-worker how to use a piece of equipment or a supervisor teaching a skill related to an individual's job. Such training might informally be termed "learning by doing."
3. *Employer-provided training:* This training is either broad or specific, depending upon the library's greater need. An example of employer-provided training might include an overall program focusing on customer service or, in an example of specific training, the nuances of a recently installed integrated materials processing or circulation system.
4. *Qualifying training:* This training is necessary to fully prepare an individual for a job. An example of qualifying training

might be an individual learning the skills necessary to satisfy core competencies for his or her job.

5. *Skill improvement training:* This training is necessary to improve an individual's performance at his or her current job. An example of skill improvement training might include attending training for a recently upgraded software program.

A well-designed staff training program can yield benefits far and above expectations by providing the following:

- Motivation
- Relevancy
- Encouragement
- Stimulation

Prior to construction of the staff training program, the library must ascertain the needs of staff and create and support a high level of "buy-in" to the program. One of the great benefits of staff who share common goals and the mission of the library is a sense of shared experience. By participating and succeeding in the training program, library staff will have a sense of accomplishment and an awareness of empoyer belief in them. Therefore, both management and staff must participate in the program. This common experience can also be employed to create the need for sustainability of the program.

Prior to embarking on a comprehensive staff training program, it will greatly benefit the library administrator to consider some basic issues:

1. How *important* is training to your library?
2. What will the *cost* be to your library to provide a comprehensive staff training program?
3. What are the *benefits* of a staff training program to your library?
4. What *kind* of training program is necessary for your library? Should it be structured in terms of centralization, decentralization (in-house or outsourced), or a combination of the two?

5. For *whom* on the staff (administration, librarians, support, some staff, all staff) will the staff training program be created?
6. If the staff training program is successful, *can it* and by what means *will it* find sustainability beyond the initial year of implementation?

When these questions have been satisfactorily answered, it is the library administrator's responsibility to create the "training" line item in the annual budget. By analyzing statistical and narrative reports regarding usage of the previous year's training offerings, the administrator must ascertain the level of funding that can be comfortably accommodated by the library's budget. An additional expense must be added to the "staff" line item in the budget as it becomes imperative for the library to engage the services of a professional.

THE ROLE OF A TRAINING ADMINISTRATOR (TA)

Although libraries may regard the appointment of a training administrator (TA) as an indulgence they cannot afford, the potential success of an overall training program and its implications on the library's staff and services suggest that such an individual is essential. Once onboard, the primary responsibility of the TA is to *create* the appropriate level of staff training program for the library. As a second duty, but one that will become the primary duty in the second year, the TA will *manage* the staff training program for the library.

A solid base of research and development experience must be utilized by the TA prior to the implementation of the training program. An experienced TA will build on previous implementations not only in libraries but also by other nonprofits. Primarily, however, as greater emphasis of late is placed on the "business" of libraries, it is essential that the TA look to the corporate sector to properly address library training issues. As a reference tool for the TA, the following publications, published by the American Society for Training and Development (ASTD), should be considered indispensable reading for planning the library's staff training program:

> *2000 Learning Outcomes Report*
> *2001 ASTD State of the Industry Report*
> *2002 ASTD State of the Industry Report**

It is also the duty of the TA to foster staff excitement for the training program. Staff can also serve to support the library administration's considerations for program sustainability. Recurring use of the program by staff will underscore the decision to implement the staff training program, thus validating its relevancy. Presenting the training program to staff through a series of positive, upbeat messages must occur on a regular basis to tout the program's fundamental merits. As the training program progresses, generating staff development and satisfaction, the workplace becomes a more cohesive institution.

The TA should establish a structure to provide the library administration with a consistent reporting mechanism designed to evaluate the program. It is critical for the library administration to understand the successes as well as the inadequacies of the training program. Accurate evaluation of the program will properly serve the specific needs of staff in succeeding years.

ESTABLISHING A FUNDING LEVEL

In order to provide sustainability for its training program, the library must consider establishing a funding level in the annual budget to support the training program equal to or greater than that currently being expended by America's most successful corporations. In 2000, according to ASTD, approximately 3.2 percent of the annual payroll of its "training investment leaders" (the top companies in America who responded to its annual survey) was

---

*All ASTD Publications may be ordered from The American Society for Training and Development, 1640 King Street, Box 1443, Alexandria, Virginia 22313-2043; telephone 800-628-2783.

budgeted for staff training.[4] However, in 2003, the clear leader in corporate staff training for the second year in a row was identified as Pfizer, Inc., with slightly greater than 15 percent of its annual payroll budgeted for staff training.[5] In a learning environment such as Pfizer, the workplace as learning place philosophy is clearly utilized to its full potential. Libraries may choose to evaluate their expected outcomes from the levels of training and learning they can achieve based on investments. It would be wise for libraries seeking to establish staff training programs to examine expected outcomes prior to creating programs, and assigning a proper budget line item to them, using the corporate percentages as noted here.

The sustainability of a successful staff training program relies on the supposition that its importance is affirmed by the library administration and therefore established as an important line item in the library's annual budget. As the atmosphere of significant change in library usage and service has become standard, a staff training program must be examined and evaluated frequently so that the annual funding level directly mirrors staff needs. The library cannot rely solely on the ebb and flow of annual grant funding cycles to maintain a staff training program beyond its initial implementation period. Sustainability of the program is imperative if the staff is to become fully engaged. The program design should seek inclusiveness and funding for at least a three-year cycle if it is to increase usability and popularity. The following checklist for sustainability should be employed when planning for the future of the program.

CHECKLIST FOR SUSTAINABILITY
OF A LIBRARY STAFF TRAINING PROGRAM

- Public expectations of library staff expertise
- Affirmed and supported by library administration
- Supported by staff
- Appropriate type of staff training designed and implemented based on need

- Continuous reporting structure
- Creation and review of appropriate level of annual funding

The overall importance of staff training can be utilized by the library to attract, hire, and retain quality staff as well as to provide customers with an elevated degree of informed customer service that is cutting-edge and exceedingly effective. A staff training program must be more than a demonstration project. It must offer library staff a means by which they can serve their library with optimum credentials and also enjoy the possibility of promotion within the library. Sustainability of the staff training program finally serves as a means by which the library maintains stability of its staff.

Chapter 2

Recruitment and Retention of Library Staff: Can These Issues Benefit from a Staff Training Program?

In a landmark white paper titled, "Recruitment, Retention and Restructuring: Human Resources in Academic Libraries," published in 2002 by the Association of College & Research Libraries (ACRL), the authors accurately contend that, "Making a profession attractive requires a mix of the right ingredients—competitive salaries, challenging jobs, a growing demand for professional expertise, respect for the profession, and long-term opportunities for growth."[1] Linking the recruitment with the retention issue, they write, "Given the increasing difficulty in recruiting MLIS graduates to academic libraries, retention of qualified and motivated employees becomes even more critical."[2]

Understanding the needs of employees at the various stages of their careers, as well as the reasons for staying with a job or seeking a new one, is one key to developing retention strategies. Academic libraries are encouraged to examine individual employee needs and consider such retention factors as "salaries and other compensation, working conditions, enrichment, and education . . . Professional development and educational opportunities can also be very effective in retaining top employees and enhancing individual job performance."[3]

Although written for academic libraries, this report includes remarks that are appropriate to every library facing these issues today; that means *every* library. If, in fact, more than one-quarter of all librarians with master's degrees will reach the age of sixty-five by 2009,[4] then a solution must be found for such a looming crisis.

RECRUITMENT

As graduate schools concentrate education efforts on training MLIS graduates increasingly fluent in information technology, the attraction of work in the private sector becomes more alluring. In addition, some librarians and information technologists are increasingly unwilling to work in direct public service, resulting in short staffing for all forms of public sector libraries.

Is a continuous program of lifelong education and staff training a cure-all for the recruitment and retention of library employees? Not entirely. However, perhaps it can serve as a single yet important element in that process.

Under an initiative supported by First Lady Laura Bush, announced in 2002, federal funding ($20 million) will be made available to libraries through the Institute of Museum and Library Services (IMLS) "for an initiative to recruit and train the next generation of librarians."[5]

With the graying of the library profession in mind and its huge potential impact on future recruitment efforts, the Public Library Association (PLA) embarked on an ambitious investigation and responded with a report including a set of short- and long-term strategies for the profession. (For an in-depth look at the complete PLA recruitment initiative titled "Report to the Executive Committee of the Public Library Association: Recruitment of Public Librarians," see <http://www.ala.org/ala/pla/projects/publiclibrecruit/recruitmentpublic.htm>.

This report is a first-rate comprehensive study of the issue. Many solid suggestions have already been implemented by a number of libraries. Still, much more needs to be done about recruitment. The Bush initiative can certainly serve as a springboard from which a national outreach strategy can be employed.

RETENTION

The retention issue, however, is a bit more difficult. In many areas of the country where professional librarians may not choose to work, future staffing (and with it, promotions) must come from within current ranks. Can a staff training program be devised to respond to the retention issue?

A number of strategies may be employed by the library to support a fully integrated or blended staff training program. Within a library-wide initiative, the library can encourage the philosophy of "partnering" with ALA-accredited library schools that

- extend training and career development opportunities;
- assist with career advancement and job placement;
- help staff grow professionally and remain current in their specialties;
- develop students who have the skills that the library will require in the future;
- incorporate accredited postgraduate courses into library-developed training plans;
- develop cosponsored formal training programs;
- support exchanges, sabbaticals, and fellowships for library staff; and
- sponsor internships, fellowships, and work-study programs for students.

Strategies to support individual staff members may include the following:

1. Developing individualized training and development programs guided by annual work plans that identify needs and opportunities in the areas of career and personal development.
2. Establishing a formal mentoring program, with high standards for admission, to give library employees broad exposure to both administrative and practical career growth.

3. Offering prescribed cross-training opportunities to ensure knowledge continuity of library issues.
4. Training younger staff to assume positions of greater responsibility.
5. Providing staff with skills to more ably perform additional tasks associated with their specialty areas.
6. Providing opportunities to learn about career options in other areas of the library.
7. Providing opportunities for teamwork.
8. Varying the kinds of training to include technical, management, business practices, library specific courses, workshops, and seminars to support job functions through a variety of delivery mechanisms.

In order to carry out these strategies successfully, the library must make a serious commitment to its training program for the viability of its own future. The expansion of library systems and academic libraries continues unabated. These institutions will have a waiting audience for their services. A knowledgeable and well-trained staff must be in place in order to fulfill those needs. Although it is understood that possible resources for training initiatives are always limited, priorities must be set based on an evaluation (using evaluation tools and the return-on-investment report) of the initiative's contributions to the library's long-term strategic goals and objectives. This evaluation must also drive the distribution of resources. Agreement must be reached on measured outcomes and the means by which to measure them.

COMPETENCY DEVELOPMENT

Development of competencies for all library positions is necessary. Core competencies are a valuable tool in determining the required skills and types of training needed for library positions. The accomplishment, through training, of these core competencies, will serve to foster greater training initiatives for those being groomed to assume greater responsibilities and advancement within their libraries. The design of a training program targeted to specific employee goals will result in greater program and individual success. Greater overall success has, of course, a greater positive impact on the library as an assimilated, performing institution. According to Paula Kaufman,

> Most of us do not need to read the spate of literature attesting to the value of continuous professional development programs. We have observed their success, and often personally benefited from them. But, professional development programs alone cannot do the job of developing individuals to take leadership roles in research libraries. They must be supplemented by, and eventually serve as supplements to, individual mentoring programs.[6]

If this is to be a successful strategy, the library employee must be provided with extremely flexible organizations. Policies will need to change; new training programs will need to be developed; different kinds of communication will be required. Careers will have to be reconceptualized and career development reinvented. The answers to the following questions ultimately will determine an organization's success:

- Is the work being done by the right people?
- Are the core tasks being done in-house and are other tasks being outsourced?
- Are the people chosen in such a way that their desires, abilities, temperaments, and assets are being matched with the demands of the tasks?
- Is everyone given the information they need to understand their part in the larger tasks?
- Does the way people are organized and managed help them complete their assignments?
- Are leaders being developed and nurtured?
- Are we identifying and mentoring our successors?[7]

Mentoring younger staff in libraries may help to ensure the future for the leadership of the profession. An excellent example of such a mentoring program may be found in the Southeast Florida

Library Information Network (SEFLIN) program called Sun Seekers. In this program, experienced library leaders currently working in libraries throughout the region mentor selected librarians and guide them through a yearlong program of training, seminars, and one-on-one discussion regarding basic areas of library management. The mission of the Sun Seekers initiative is

> To develop and enhance the leadership skills of library staff through participation in a program that will provide the opportunity for individuals to be better prepared to create, articulate and contribute to the vitality, growth and success of the library profession.[8]

The objectives of the program are identified as:

1. To develop librarians who have leadership potential as leaders of 21st century libraries.
2. To develop a cadre of mentors who will act as guides, coaches and role models.
3. To provide a high quality leadership program for emerging library leaders which will instill progressive and effective leadership strategies, attitudes and skills by:
   - encouraging participants to recognize and/or initiate innovations, seize opportunities and take risks where appropriate; and
   - guiding participants to appreciate and thrive in a changing political and demographic environment.
4. To serve as a mechanism for continuing leadership development among Sun Seekers alumni and a broad based library leadership network.[9]

More than just adequate preparation of library leadership, intensive mentoring, viewed as a continuing education opportunity, is imperative to ensure that the leadership of the library profession receives a constant infusion of talented people in the future. Programs such as Sun Seekers take a giant step in that direction.

Chapter 3

Suggestions for a Comprehensive Training Program for Library Staff

Many librarians have inadequate knowledge, skills, and proficiency in basic and advanced computer applications, management, and library topics. Librarians must work and be successful in rapidly changing environments. To be successful in the twenty-first century, librarians must take full advantage of the wealth of education and training delivered through a variety of technology-based methods. In direct response to the national need for an innovative technology-based continuing education and training program for librarians, this proposal may be used as an accessible and flexible program of hands-on learning for librarians.

A comprehensive training program for library staff should directly address priorities to employ inventive methods to achieve an integrated program of education and training, to train librarians to improve customers' capability of using information successfully, and to instruct librarians in the methods of outcome-based evaluation practices.

The success of lifelong learning for librarians depends upon an accessible, flexible, and easy-to-use connection between the learner and education and training opportunities. This connection must be clearly established between librarians and the use of technology in advancing skills and specializations. Technology-based training must support not only core competencies essential for librarians to perform their jobs better but also improved services to both internal and external library customers.

In order to further these goals, librarians in all types of libraries and communities must acquire a heightened awareness of the value of technology-based learning. Successfully serving library customers requires a program of lifelong learning to acquire and maintain a wide range of skills. These skills must support librarians in successfully assisting library users and other library staff in a coherent and knowledgeable manner and effectively manage a changing library environment. Therefore, it is imperative that librarians receive a high-quality, readily available program of continuous and lifelong learning. Librarians also must be given the opportunity to improve their technology knowledge and skills.

COMPONENTS

The key outcomes of a comprehensive training program for library staff must include the following:

- A "needs assessment" survey would be administered to the staff.
- A regular reporting mechanism would provide monthly usage statistics to the library director. The reports for the library must include usage statistics and estimates of actual "market value" of each training session delivered.
- An evaluation survey or other survey mechanism would be used to assess the overall program and its components of library staff who had participated in a comprehensive training program for library staff (See Chapter 8).
- Sample of program goals and objectives
    Librarians would learn to assess training needs and deliver technology-based continuing education and training to meet those needs.
    Librarians would enhance critical skills and specializations through a comprehensive curriculum of technology, management, and library-specific courses.
    Librarians would develop an understanding of the benefits and outcomes of a technology-based continuing education and training program.

Librarians would understand the important role of technology-based training in providing lifelong learning opportunities for library staff.

Library researchers would conduct evaluation activities that
facilitate the design of the training content, inform the
training program planning activities, and assess the impact
and outcomes of the training program on librarians and the
libraries that they serve.

Program partners would be trained in outcome-based evaluation of continuing education and training programs.

Reproducibility

A new study by the American Society for Training and Development (ASTD) and The MASIE Center (titled "The Learning
Technology Acceptance Study: If We Build It, Will They Come?")
revealed that 38 percent of employees polled from seven Fortune
500 companies said they preferred e-learning to classroom training. Most indicated they were satisfied with their e-learning expe-
riences, learned what they needed faster than through classroom
training, and were willing to take additional e-learning courses in
the future.

According to a white paper titled, "Profiting from Learning: Do
Firms' Investments in Education and Training Pay Off?" written
by Laurie J. Bassi, Jens Ludwig, Daniel P. McMurrer, and Mark
Van Buren,

> direct costs for training at U.S. firms typically amount to 2
> percent of payroll, while indirect and opportunity costs may
> raise the total to 10 percent or more. Adding to this, the costs
> of investments in *informal* training are likely to be at least as
> large as investments made in formal programs.[1]

The U.S. corporate training model suggests that the continuing
education and training of librarians in all types of libraries and
communities should be approached in a similar manner. Therefore, in an effort to provide librarians with a comparable climate of
continuous learning delivered through technology, a comprehen-

sive training program for library staff would provide librarians with technology-based training in order to establish learning environments that advance their skills and specializations. The program could demonstrate that the program can be replicated in any library environment.

Establishing Consistent Needs

Establishing accessible, flexible, and easy-to-use training programs for librarians is one of the most important library initiatives of the twenty-first century. The challenge of continuously training librarians to successfully negotiate their way through the digital information environment, effectively and efficiently manage libraries, and serve an increasingly demanding public must be addressed. In reviewing the training needs of librarians, it is fair to state the following needs:

- Librarians need training at every skill level to acquire the knowledge necessary to successfully use constantly changing computer hardware and software.
- Librarians need training in managing technology to successfully plan and operate library information systems, networks, and electronic information resources.
- Librarians need knowledge and skills on using the Internet and developing and maintaining library-based Web services.
- A selective number of librarians need highly developed knowledge and skills on planning, implementing, maintaining, and supporting library and information systems critical to the successful operations of libraries including training labs, networks, and Internet services.
- A selective number of librarians need highly developed knowledge and skills in management in order to more efficiently and effectively lead and operate libraries.
- Librarians need continuous education on library-specific topics so they can advance library services and proactively address issues affecting libraries and library customers.

- Librarians need training that is delivered in accessible, flexible, and easy-to-use methods.

Adaptability

In small and large, rural and urban libraries, librarians must work and be successful in rapidly changing technological, political, and service environments. Librarians must begin taking full advantage of the wealth of training available through a variety of technology-based delivery systems including the Web, teleconferencing, streaming media, and satellite delivery.

A comprehensive training program for library staff satisfies the learning needs of public, academic, school, and special librarians located in urban, suburban, and rural areas. Successfully training librarians in these diverse environments demonstrates the viability of technology-based training as a national model for delivering lifelong learning for librarians.

Designing Curriculum

The library collaboratively develops a training curriculum provided *through* and *within* a technologically driven environment. Four major education and training areas are targeted, containing both self-study and instructor-led classes that cover the critically important areas of computer applications, advanced information technology, management, and library-specific topics.

- *Computer applications:* This training is delivered through a combination of Web-based applications and instructor-led training. The Web-based training module will deliver courses including the most popular desktop applications used by librarians.
- *Advanced information technology:* This Web-based training module delivers high-end information and technologically rich courses for librarians supporting library and information systems and services.
- *Management:* This Web-based training module delivers courses on assessing performance, program management, leadership,

business writing, communications, finance, human resources, leadership, personal development, program management, customer services, and team building.

- *Library specific:* This training module provides university- and professional-level courses delivered to librarians through a variety of technology (satellite, videoconferences, streaming media, and, Web based) on library-related issues.

Management Plan Program Coordination

A comprehensive training program for library staff is managed by a lead training administrator. Supporting training administrators in the case of a large library system with multiple branches are necessary. The duties of the lead training administrator are as follows:

- Leading the technology training team; serving as lead training administrator and communications liaison to local training administrators (as necessary)
- Conducting literature searches on technology training
- Coordinating the identification, study, and selection of technology training vendors/agencies
- Managing the implementation and daily operations of the program
- Drafting, reviewing, and writing grants and reports
- Developing, hosting, and managing a program Web site that would include all of the reports, surveys, assessments, and evaluation data regarding a comprehensive training program for library staff (In addition, comprehensive information would be provided for access to all program classes, courses, and supporting materials in the four areas of training.)

BUDGET ISSUES

A comprehensive training program for library staff provides a cost-effective model for delivering continuing education and training to librarians in all types of libraries and communities.

In order to conduct the business of the program, applicant and partners incur program-related expenses including office supplies, photocopying, postage, and long-distance calls and faxes between program team members, the advisory committee, and others.

Successfully providing continuing education and training for librarians is based on a commitment by library administration to provide staff training days for librarians to take classes. Libraries participating in a comprehensive training program for library staff grant each participating librarian five staff training days per year to take classes offered through the program.

"In-kind" contributions in the form of staff training days are based on following calculations: Librarians per year take computer applications, management, and library-specific classes. The library provides five training days per year × average librarian salary ($20 × 7.5 hours × 5 days = $750/librarian per year)

PROGRAM EVALUATION

The program evaluation will be planned and implemented by the library. The evaluation component to the program relies on both formative and summative evaluation approaches to determine both program outputs and outcomes. At the end of the program, the program team conducts a summative evaluation to determine the degree to which the program accomplished its goals. To conduct the summative evaluation, the program team engages in a number of approaches (e.g., surveys, focus groups, interviews) to assess the impact and outcomes of the technology and other training curriculum on participants. The results from the summative evaluation will be part of the library's annual report.

In particular, the evaluation component of the program

- conducts a training needs assessment for the participating partners/libraries prior to the selection of course modules;
- develop a training module plan based on the findings of the needs assessment activities;

- conducts a skills pretest of participating librarians to determine baseline technology skills of participants;
- develops a training outcomes assessment evaluation tool/set to determine the impact of the training on the participating librarians as well as the libraries in which they serve; and
- conducts a skills posttest of participants after participation in the training program to determine growth in competencies of participants.

Throughout the program, the library employs a number of formative evaluation techniques to determine program outputs. The library administrators serve in an evaluation capacity and provide regular feedback and review of program documents and activities. Also, there are a number of activities built into the method for the program team to obtain feedback and suggestions from program partners, training participants, and others.

DISSEMINATION

The library develops, hosts, and manages a Web site that is accessible to anyone with a Web browser. All of the reports, surveys, assessments, and evaluation data regarding a comprehensive training program for library staff should be available on the site. In addition, a comprehensive training program for library staff provides comprehensive information about and a central site for access to all program classes, courses, and supporting materials in the four areas of targeted training.

SUSTAINABILITY

A comprehensive training program for library staff is sustainable because it is accessible, easy to use, technology-based, affordable, and scalable. Using a variety of available and simple technology provides librarians with unlimited access on a twenty-four-hour basis to hundreds of Web-based courses. Using one password per librarian per training module allows the specific needs of librarians to be precisely matched and funded. The availability of a comprehensive continuing education and training program directly supports the library in attracting, hiring, and retaining quality staff. The learning outcomes of such a program include improved services for library customers.

Libraries cannot rely solely on yearly grant funding to deliver a successful continuing education and training program beyond its initial demonstration. Libraries cannot run the risk of such a so-called anywhere/anytime library staff training program declining into a nowhere/no place staff training program. Time must be set aside for training. The best service possible will not be attainable if there is a downward spiral of indifference to training.

The sustainability of a successful staff training program relies on its affirmed importance by library administration by providing librarians with leave time for training, as well as its place as an important line item in the library's annual budget. As significant change in library usage and service has become the standard, a continuing education and training program for librarians must be frequently examined and evaluated so that the annual funding level directly mirrors staff needs.

Chapter 4

The Workplace As Learning Place

Whether one employs the words *seamless, incorporated, blended,* or *integrated,* the concept of *learning* for library staff should be seen as equal to the concept of *working.* For too long, organizations have spent an inordinate amount of time trying to design training programs for staff that stand apart from daily work. In order for this concept to be accepted as the norm, there must be no difference between the two.

It is a given that staff must attend training. Often, they must leave the workplace, sometimes for several hours, sometimes an entire day, to do so. At other times, staff is expected to participate in the library's training program on personal time. Given the obvious drawbacks to this, including the library's operating hours, in which the library is often open seven days a week including evenings, and pervasive short staffing, finding time for such offsite training can be challenging. Still, with change remaining a constant in a field where technology has become the driving force, continuous training must not be seen as separate from the work.

"Does learning look and feel like work, and does work look and feel like learning?"[1] This question cuts both ways. If the library encourages continuous education and training and supports a comprehensive learning environment while dealing with the challenges of simply keeping its doors open and providing service, then the integration of learning into the workplace can be accomplished. However, if, on the other hand, the workplace stifles further education and training, frowns upon new technology that supports better customer service, or worse, ignores it altogether, then the opportunity to create a progressive atmosphere does not occur.

STEPS IN CREATING
AN INTEGRATED LEARNING ENVIRONMENT

1. Core competencies must be produced to provide guidelines in order to "frame" the knowledge and skills necessary to be met by each library employee.
2. The library must maintain an atmosphere where continuous learning is promoted and supported.
3. The library must encourage staff to incorporate learning into daily activities and to share learning with colleagues.
4. Regardless of the specific learning tool (e.g., Web based, instructor led, computer based, teleconference, compressed video) and whether or not that tool is an individual learning experience or group experience (e.g., seminar, workshop), the environment itself must be viewed as one that supports and sustains the overall program of continuous learning.
5. The library must be in the position of purchasing and maintaining the materials (software, hardware, connectivity) necessary for staff to utilize learning in the workplace.
6. There must be learning leaders or "champions" selected from the library staff who will serve as visible symbols of the library's commitment to the continuous learning environment.
7. There must be staff selected as trainers who can serve as in-house experts recognized by the staff and utilized for individual support when necessary.

"BLENDED LEARNING"
TO KEEP THE STAFF ENGAGED

Every few months a new trend hits the training industry. One of the latest trends revolves around the application of blended learning solutions. The idea behind blended learning is that instructional designers review a learning program, divide it into modules, and determine the best medium to deliver those modules to the learner. Various media include but are not limited to technologies such as the following:

- Traditional classroom or lab settings
- Reading assignments
- CD-ROM
- Performance support tools
- Teletraining
- Stand-alone Web-based training
- Asynchronous Web-based training
- Synchronous Web-based training[2]

Many avenues are available to receive training that a student may pick and choose those he or she is willing to accept as the most appropriate means for him or her.

Although online training, through Web-based and desktop delivery, is a relatively recent phenomenon in the library training milieu, it has been used in the corporate environment long enough for a solid base of user statistics to develop that points out where and how this form of delivery is being employed. According to a report titled, *2002 State of the Industry: ASTD's Annual Review of Trends in Employer-Provided Training in the United States,* published by the American Society for Training and Development, e-learning has returned to its highest level of use since 1997:

> Last year's survey showed that the average percentage of training delivered via learning technologies in ASTD's Benchmarking Service had stalled. . . . In this year's survey, this figure edged up [to] its highest since [that] reported in 1997. . . . [W]e believe that 2000 marked a new era of growth for e-learning. These signs of new life have only been amplified by the events of 2001. Cutbacks on travel and the need for security have led more organizations to increase than decrease their e-learning since September 11, 2001.[3]

WHAT ARE THE LATEST TRENDS?

Also, according to the ASTD report, the latest trends "affecting workplace learning and training" are listed here in order of importance. This listing combines responses from both the private and public sectors of the marketplace, yet is equally as relevant to the library community.

- Money
- Diversity
- Time
- Work (in new ways, e.g., "virtual")
- World changes
- Meaning
- Pace of change
- Knowledge
- Technology
- Challenging the traditional notion of a career[4]

With computers occupying the desktops of most library staff, sufficient opportunity to use these computers to undergo training online during downtime (on the rare occurrence that there is downtime) exists. The concept is sound, although evidence suggests that most library staff availing themselves of online learning are generally gaining that knowledge at home, rather than on the job.

Accepting the notion that learning equals work implies that staff are working at home by engaging in online learning while away from the workplace. However, in an era where more and more of us are taking work home to increase our knowledge and skills, becoming involved in learning at home is simply a means by which we increase our employability. This requires us to go the extra mile, so to speak, and work harder at learning so we can employ that learning at work, thus integrating the two entities. "E-learning, distance education, computer-based training, Web-based training, or distributed learning. Whatever you call it, e-learning is creating quite a stir in corporate America and becoming a growth industry in the education and training field."[5]

With an estimate of 55 percent of corporate learning expected by staff in 2002,[6] the library community may well soon surpass that figure. After all, the technology that has become so pervasive in the library workplace ought to lend itself to more and more staff becoming comfortable with the medium as a primary learning delivery method.

One of the primary benefits of e-learning in an asynchronous learning environment is the flexibility it offers the learner. The value of the asynchronous learning network (ALN) atmosphere is flexibility for the participants of the library training program; its philosophy of access also supports the workplace as learning place environment. Such flexibility supports staff motivation to learn. Creating such an environment establishes a climate of trust between administration and staff, a concern that is vital to staff retention in libraries.

Chapter 5

Train the Trainer:
The In-House Training Opportunity

When the library is ready to hire a training administer (TA), library training assistant (LTA), or library trainer (LT), an experienced individual may be sought who has worked in the private sector. If this is the route decided upon by the library administration, a learning curve will be needed for the individual to familiarize himself or herself with the library environment. On a certain level be some comparisons may be brought by experienced trainers to the library environment, but specific aspects of establishing the training model may be quite different. For the corporate trainer unfamiliar with the rhythm of the library and unaccustomed to its idiosyncrasies, he or she may simply not be an appropriate fit for the position.

On the other hand, since a parallel issue to retention supports the "grow your own" philosophy, current in-house library staff may be already equipped with the proper tools to make midcareer adjustments to serve the library better as an in-house trainer. Most training, after all, is delivered not by professional trainers but by experienced and technically capable employees who are called upon to train their colleagues in their area of expertise. Therefore, the library may be better positioned, both philosophically and financially, to seek fulfillment for the position of library trainer from within its own ranks. Through retraining and enrollment in a comprehensive course of study resulting in the receipt of a training certification, the library may be wise to encourage a member of its own staff to seek out this position.

Creating a new position may be a luxury for many libraries experiencing budget issues. However, it may be less costly to create a cadre of in-house trainers than it would be to outsource these tasks. It would certainly be worthwhile for the budget-strapped library to investigate establishing the position and filling it from within. Once an individual is identified, however, the library must also be willing to support the necessary training for the selected individual and then train others who wish to carry the training banner further.

TRAINING PROGRAMS

Training programs for certification vary in the time and financial investment affecting both the individual and the library. However, it is money well spent considering that the investment will be dedicated to building the library's training infrastructure. For example, The Training Clinic (visit <http://www.thetrainingclinic. com>), a learning professional training organization, offers the following training programs to support a variety of training pursuits such as: certified e-training facilitator, certified technical training specialist, presentation skills certificate (Microsoft approved), certified training presenter, certified instructional systems designer, certified training manager, certified training administrator, certified orientation specialist, and certified master trainer. The Training Clinic bases its courses of instruction on competencies for training and development professionals recommended by the American Society for Training and Development (ASTD) and the International Board of Standards for Training (IBST), performance and instruction. The Training Clinic's course content for these certificates is matched to the suggested skills and competencies of both organizations. The most significant aspect of these training workshops for libraries is that they are designed for those with training responsibility. This suggests there *are* individuals who have not received professional certification or even workshop training prior to being selected as in-house trainers. Suddenly they find themselves saddled with responsibility and need to become experts at the speed of light.

In order to provide viability for the trainer, receiving a certification can serve a useful function. However, for the motivated trainer on a strict budget, the ASTD offers a wealth of published information through its Web site (<www.astd.org>) and in numerous publications (books and articles). In addition, a considerable amount of material is published annually on the subject of training the trainer. A highly selected bibliography of this material may be found in the Selected Training Bibliographies section of this book. However, a simple directed search of the literature will yield a substantial quantity of material to support the trainer's learning base of knowledge.

In order to be effective, the library's train-the-trainer module ought to include a number of goals. These include the potential trainers' ability to understand and promote the following:

- Understand principles of learning
- Develop objectives
- Plan lessons
- Identify how people think, learn, assimilate, and retain information
- Evaluate whether learning has taken place
- Generate discussion
- Ask the right questions
- Solve problems
- Use modern presentation skills and techniques
- Evaluate and critique existing training methods

ENGAGING THE LEARNER

Although training styles vary, a primary principle of successful training is to engage the learner. Engaging those who will become in-house trainers is as important as the means by which these same trainers will train their own classes. How does one successfully accomplish this?

According to Basil Deming, program manager at The Graduate School, United States Department of Agriculture in Washington, DC, there are ten steps to engaging the learner.

1. Determine what's in it for them.
2. Ask participants what they want to learn from the instruction, then clarify and determine their expectations.
3. Probe frequently.
4. Encourage application.
5. Test and give feedback.
6. Start with questions.
7. Run counter to expectations.
8. Start with what learners know.
9. Use visual modes—use humor.
10. Provide an advanced organizer.[1]

The library has found its skilled, trained, and engaging in-house trainer. In agreeing to support a sustainable train-the-trainer module, the library enters into the program with the understanding that the individual selected to serve as the library's first in-house trainer will be the key to its success. The program will only be as good as its participants and the outcome will become visible as the formal training program begins; as others learn from this individual, they will then have the skills and knowledge to present this training to others. For a selected listing of train-the-trainer degrees, certificates, workshops, and courses, see Appendix B.

Chapter 6

The Conference As a Continuing Education Opportunity

Too often, library staff are sent off to conferences under the generic budget line item of "staff development." However, if viewed from the perspective of the continuing education trainer, the professional conference can serve as a means by which library staff glean more continuing education in a few days than possible in numerous half-day workshops over the course of some months. A national conference may offer a plethora of papers, presentations, hands-on skill workshops, philosophical arguments over issues, and, not an inconsiderable expenditure of time, meetings with library vendors. There are many reasons for attending a conference and approaching it as a continuing education activity. However, "two of the best reasons for attending a conference or seminar have nothing to do with the topic or formal sessions."[1]

REASONS TO ATTEND A CONFERENCE OR SEMINAR

Networking

The first is the networking potential from the contacts made with other attendees. Few things will provide as good a reference source as a good network of contacts in the field. Cultivating and maintaining these contacts is one of the best reasons for attending a conference. A safety or environmental professional's job can be a lonely position in many organizations. Often, few internal personnel are available with whom to discuss plans and programs to get opinions. A network of outside contacts can fill this gap.

Planning can extend to networking as well. List several challenges currently being faced at work. Who is likely to be at the conference that may provide useful information in helping with these challenges? For seminars, this list should be more specific. Prepare a detailed list of questions regarding the specific topic of the seminar. Keep the list handy during the seminar as a reminder to ask any questions that the general presentation does not answer. Make appointments to visit with key contacts who will be attending the event or who are located in the area of the event. It may be beneficial to research other resources located in the area where the event will be held.

Escape from the Work Environment

The second reason is the value of getting away from the work environment. This author does not mean to view attendance at a seminar or conference as a vacation; it is not. The focus should still be on safety or environmental issues, but absent are the day-to-day pressures of constant phone calls and demands for attention that are present in the workplace. This escape aspect can also affect perspective. Dealing with the same work situations day after day, we can lose our ability to distinguish the important from the insignificant. The revitalizing experience of a conference or seminar with professional peers can remind us why we went into the safety/environmental profession in the first place. This can lead to gains in performance when returning to work, even if nothing new was learned at the event. Remember, time spent talking with others in the hall is at least as important as time spent in formal sessions.[2]

It is wise for individuals to adopt a structural approach to conference attendance. An individual must plan a comprehensive approach to attendance so that he or she can maximize the experience and so that both the individual and the library gain something from it. Preplanning is the key to a successful conference experience.

PLANNING FOR THE CONFERENCE

If the concept of conference attendance is viewed as a continuing education opportunity, the CE program manager may consider the use of a conference template to be employed by an individual attending a conference. This template would serve to capture specific information regarding specific sessions attended at the conference, so that the information can be shared with the appropriate colleagues who may not have had the opportunity to attend. For an annual or a special library-related conference where many sessions may be attended, this template may be copied in multiples to be filled out and distributed on a variety of topics. The template might resemble the form found in Box 6.1.

Authors Claire M. Kilian and Dawn Hukai offer a number of tips regarding the preplanning by the individual heading off to a conference:

- Think about why you are attending
- Plan ahead for follow-up
- Use the speaker or attendee list for contacts
- Don't forget your business cards

Then, when you are there:

- Increase your base of contacts
- Use the proceedings to identify sessions that best meet your needs
- Maintain concentration and persistence
- Gain perspective

Finally, after you return:

- Bring what you've learned back to the library to share with colleagues
- Consider posting summaries of what you have learned
- Share notes and ideas with those whom you interact with daily
- Experiment using the knowledge gained from the conference experience[3]

BOX 6.1. Library Conference Participation

Library conference: _____

Session/workshop title and topic: _____

Date: _____

Session/workshop presenter(s): _____

Session/workshop presenter(s) telephone/e-mail: _____

Presenter affiliation: _____

Presenter Web site: _____

Key points of session/workshop:

    1. _____

    2. _____

    3. _____

Relevance to you or your library:

    1. _____

    2. _____

    3. _____

General overall comments: _____

_____

_____

Who else in your library would benefit from this report? List appropriate individual(s) or department(s). _____

Evaluate the presenter on a scale of 1 (low) to 5 (high):

Presentation skills: _____ Subject expertise: _____

Your name: _____

Telephone/e-mail: _____

Handouts of interest are attached to this report. ☐Yes ☐No

SELECTED CONFERENCES

On the national scene, the American Library Association annual conference is the largest event organized for librarians in the world. More than 25,000 librarians, library staff, trustees, and others gather in a selected city each year.

ALA divisions, round tables and committees present more than 250 programs and pre-conferences on a wide variety of topics. Hundreds of companies showcase the latest information products and services. In addition, three ALA divisions—the American Association of School Librarians (AASL), Association of College & Research Libraries (ACRL) and the Public Library Association (PLA)—offer separate national conference programs and exhibits for their members. The Association for Library Service to Children (ALSC), the Association for Library Trustees and Advocates (ALTA) and the Reference User Services Association (RUSA) jointly offer biannual national institutes that focus on continuous education for members, trustees and other professionals to keep them updated on trends in librarianship. The Library Information and Technology Association (LITA) also offers an annual national institute.[4]

In addition, the Library Administration and Management Association (LAMA), the Association for Library Collections and Technical Services (ALCTS), and the Young Adult Library Services Association (YALSA) also offer extensive programs at the annual conference, among other specialties.

Regardless of the state or the activity, the group will usually be represented by a conference. Individuals may visit the annual and updated listing of regional conferences in order to ascertain if they may wish to attend one for the purpose of a concentrated continuing education opportunity. This list may be viewed by visiting "ALA Conference Planning Calendar 2002-2012" at <http://www.ala.org/cro/state_calendar.html>.

RECEIVING CONTINUING EDUCATION CREDIT

The concept of obtaining continuing education for conference attendance is an activity that is valued by an increasing number of university, college, and school libraries. More and more non-degree programs, including conferences, are considered eligible for continuing education units (CEUs). CEUs were created as a way to document noncredit work in specifically developed activities for adult learners in a variety of disciplines. As an example of an institution of higher education taking a proactive view regarding CEUs and conference attendance, the University of Baltimore has established, in their training and professional development program, a means by which the university would partner with a professional organization to offer CEUs for staff attending a conference.

CEUs are extremely important to academic library staff because they are gained in order to retain existing certification or to recertify their professional certificates.

The Oklahoma Department of Libraries sanctions this policy. Its statement regarding this issue reads as follows:

> It is the vision of the Oklahoma Library Association and the Oklahoma Department of Libraries that public libraries in this state be administered and staffed by trained personnel. The Oklahoma Department of Libraries and the Oklahoma Library Association believe that the library staff must increase their skills and knowledge through continuing education in order to keep abreast of developments in the information age. This, in turn, upgrades the library profession, enriches the individual librarian and promotes quality library service.[5]

Clearly, if continuing education units are available to library staff who attend conferences, then there are dual reasons to attend: the importance of spending time with peers networking and participating in professional programs and receiving credits to enhance one's skills and knowledge.

Chapter 7

The ROI Report and E-Training

MEASURING THE BENEFITS OF E-TRAINING

E-training, that is, training coursework, workshops, and seminars delivered either online or by computer, is increasingly integrated into staff training programs in libraries. Does a means exist by which the library can gauge whether a positive return on its investment (ROI) was gained through its staff training program, specifically the component delivered through e-training? If so, what is the appropriate tool that should be employed to measure the program's success? The answer is the return-on-investment (ROI) report.

First, let us assume that a library has created a set of core competencies for all library staff positions. Inherent in these core competencies is a mandatory obligation by staff to satisfy certain continuing education and training components prior to their receiving either positive annual reviews or to seek advancement. The library has taken its first step toward creating an organization-wide continuing education and training program for its staff.

The library administration has guaranteed the implementation of its training program by including a line item in the annual budget to fund the program. That line item, as recommended by the most successful companies in the private sector, is equal to approximately 5 percent of the library's annual total salary expenditure. A training administrator (TA) or training team (if the library is a larger system) has been named by the library. All of the decisions have been made regarding the *level* of training needed based upon the results of a needs assessment survey conducted by the library

TA. The TA has recommended specific areas of concentration that will constitute the staff training program. How, then, will training be delivered to the library staff?

Discussions have been held to determine how much training will be delivered through e-training methods. In whatever manner the training is delivered, numerous forms of technological components will be associated with it. What will be delivered via videotape, teleconferences, streaming media, Webcasts, CD-ROM, DVD, or a newer technology just entering the marketplace? As flexibility is desirable in the number and type of courses, seminars, workshops, etc. that are offered, e-training is clearly the means by which a number of training competencies will be fulfilled.

Today, an increasing volume of training is available to libraries on the Web, from strictly desktop application courses to professional management courses, to high-end information technology courses to library-specific courses offering training on a variety of library-related issues for every level of employee.

E-training also offers the flexibility of scheduling, which, in an era of short staffing and longer working hours is vital to the success of a library training program. E-training is convenient for staff taking courses, accessing the individual lessons of a course, or even repeating parts of a course. Learning styles differ, and e-training may not be suited to everyone. In fact, no more than one-third of the library staff may be expected to participate in a regular program of e-training. The other two-thirds may prefer traditional learning styles, in which they can learn in a group led by an instructor. For this group, the allure of training's social component remains an attractive feature of the learning process. However, given the nature of library staffing it is unlikely that this luxury will persist. After all, instructor-led training usually requires staff to either leave the workplace entirely or at least leave their desks in order to participate. Therefore, if only for the reason of practicality itself, e-training, by necessity, will gain increased support as a training style in libraries.

Since training is now *required* in our theoretical library, how will accountability be measured? Libraries must find a means to evaluate and maximize the value of their *human* assets. How does the library measure its return on investment of a staff training program? Since e-training is a recent phenomenon in libraries, justification may be required. If this is the case, then the ROI report is the appropriate and defensible instrument for such measurement. According to training specialist Patricia Pulliam Phillips, accountability is not isolated to one sector, one industry, or one type of program any longer. Its importance is engendered in organizations and programs of all types. However, the actual implementation of accountability processes is still in its infancy in many sectors.[1] The library world is just one such sector where the consideration of justification of expenditures by virtue of an ROI report is starting to emerge.

In every corner of the training and development field, the pressure to measure the return on investment is intensifying. At some time or another, virtually every library will, undoubtedly, face this important issue. Whether in the private or public sector, providers of e-training specifically and training in general are coming under greater scrutiny and, therefore, additional demand to issue return-on-investment data. Bottom lines are scrutinized so thoroughly these days, even in nonprofit organizations where there appears not even to be a *visible* bottom line, that ROI will emerge as a mandatory element in cost-benefit analysis.

WHAT IS ROI?

The term *return on investment* started as a standard *accounting* practice and evolved into a means by which a cost-benefit may be realized. In the case of training, the library administration may ask, what is the direct benefit received by introducing an e-training program into the library? A gross oversimplification might well pose the question, "if we pay for it, what will we get out of it?"

Once the value of creating such a report is understood, a set of questions regarding the library's training expectations must be determined prior to ascertain the ROI.

- How does my service delivery compare to other libraries?
- In what specific areas are libraries providing training?
- What value does the library's investment in training provide?

- What targets should I set for my value return?
- How can I best communicate the value of library staff training?

A return-on-investment report can be as simple as discerning if trained employees can perform their jobs better upon the conclusion of a specific training activity; or it can be designed as a complicated, economically based metrics report breaking down cost benefits into targeted, measured, and graded percentages. ROI reports are particularly useful in the following areas.

1. Helping library managers prioritize investment by providing hard numbers to compare investment options. For example, if possible it may be wiser for the library to negotiate an e-training contract with an outside vendor than to create courses from scratch. Although the price of software packages (such as Blackboard and WebCT) used for creating unique e-training courses have decreased sharply, the cost benefit of simply purchasing a vendor-created course will still be more favorable. There are many staff hours involved in creating unique courses and the learning curve necessary for mastering the courseware can be somewhat daunting.

2. Setting a program design threshold for e-training projects that deliver ROIs of at least 200 percent, wherever possible. For example, the library should set its sights higher when the expectation of ROI on e-training is designed. Although an intangible, such as whether the training helped staff to better perform their duties thus providing a higher level of customer service in the library, may be measured using a variety of survey tools, the ROI report can still be valuable in delivering the hard numbers related to direct investment measurement of that intangible.

3. Imposing some discipline on the part of vendors and decision makers to support business impact claims by taking a more methodical and quantifiable approach to business justification. For example, one of the most difficult issues in contracting an outside vendor to train library staff is the inability to obtain quality statistical reporting from that vendor. The vendor assumes the library will collect such data on its own or that the library will be willing

to pay extra for the vendor to create such a service outside its primary contractual obligations. It would be wise, then, to hold the vendor responsible for collecting and delivering appropriate statistical data so that they may be available to the library for the ROI report. A considerable cost savings will result in a positive ROI report.

Some e-training project justifications are based on cost savings alone where the cost of traditional training is compared to the cost of e-training. In an *integrated* training program, where traditional training deliverables such as instructor-led and video training are combined with e-training deliverables, the cost savings will vary. However, it is more likely that the cost of "packaged" e-training products will cost less than "live" instructor-led training products because the logistical aspects of the latter often include transportation of instructor, hotel accommodations, meals, car rentals for the instructor, and so on.

Direct and Indirect Costs

The ROI report should include a mechanism for forecasting the actual expected benefits, converted to monetary values, and then comparison of benefits to the projected cost. In order to determine the cost of the library e-training program, it would be preferable to separate the expected costs into *direct* and *indirect* categories. Most *direct* costs will come from equipment, such as computer hardware, software, and staff costs. Staff costs include the salaries and wages of anyone who works to provide the program. Staff costs should also include benefits paid to staff such as medical insurance and retirement. Benefits are at least 28 percent of salaries but can often be higher. *Indirect* costs are costs of overall library operations which can be allocated to the e-training program. They include things such as custodial service, utility costs, security, landscaping, and other overhead expenses. Indirect costs may also include the cost of the facility and an overall administration fee to the library. This fee can range anywhere from between 20 to 50 percent or higher, depending on the institution.

"Hard" vs. "Soft" ROI Reports

In preparing the ROI report, the library must also consider whether it is better positioned to submit a "hard" ROI report wherein the expenditure of funds proves that it can generate a specific return in a measured amount of time, or a "soft" ROI report that offers expected assurances to enhance efficiency or customer satisfaction. If the library intends to determine the financial value rather than simply the costs of library training, market values may be based strictly on the market value of the training and product services being purchased for the program. For example, if an *integrated* staff training program has been designed to deliver a combination self-study, instructor-led, and technologically delivered training products, then a close analysis of products and services purchased to support the program can be designed to determine the actual cost *and* the market value of the staff training program.

TWO SUGGESTED EXAMPLES OF THE ROI FORMULA

Example One

Once a library has laid the groundwork it can apply a ROI formula. Training ROI formulas vary, but here is a suggested one that may include the following general categories:

- Product data elements (specific e-training products purchased for the program)
- Cost categories (direct/indirect)
- Market value key (based upon the actual cost of products in the open marketplace)
- Program objectives
- Communications targets (overall promotion, e-mails, informational meetings, newsletter, Web site, moderated forum)
- Methods of measuring effectiveness (surveys, focus groups, interviews, case studies)
- Tangible/intangible benefits (expected outcomes)

- Effect of influences on program (geographic, time constraints, access to technology, seasonal fluctuations, motivation, profession isolation, attitudes toward e-training)
- Satisfaction measurement (on employee, management, library, customer)

When this information has been ascertained, consider calculating the statistical data using the following steps:

Step 1. Add the costs of the training period for design and development, promotion, administration, delivery (staff or technology), materials, facilities, employee wages, lost productivity, and evaluation.

Step 2. Calculate the benefits, including labor savings, productivity increases, potential income generation, new services, and other cost savings such as lower maintenance, turnover, and debt costs.

Step 3. Divide benefits by costs to get the ROI.

A prototypical report can also resemble an exhaustive spreadsheet, complete with drop down menus allowing users to add and subtract factors that could affect the outcomes of the program, including implementation cost overruns, staff reductions, and improvements in technological dependability.

Example Two

The ROI report could also include data elements that simply outline the costs of traditional classroom training as opposed to e-training. Such an analysis would include the following data elements:

- Wages of trainees for one week of training (500 employees @ ?/hr)
- Travel costs (50 percent of people traveling)
- Trainer wages
- Trainer travel
- Development costs (custom training)
- Delivery systems (library computers)

This example might better be employed when library managers have been requested to produce a ROI report *prior* to spending the money on a project, rather than simply using it as a yardstick for spending after the project is complete. It all depends on the level of sophistication expected by the library.

PRACTICAL ELEMENTS FOR CALCULATING ROI

The following are several things a library can do to lay the groundwork for calculating and securing positive, accurate, and persuasive ROI. Consider the solution. Before committing to training, identify the challenge and make certain training is the best solution. For example, if the problem is poor customer service, perhaps an ongoing series of sensitivity-training workshops may be more appropriate rather than a full-blown skills training program.

1. *Get a baseline.* To calculate training benefits, quantify the *before* environment. Measure everything that training might improve. For example, if training employees about sexual harassment, review the number of employees, any filed lawsuits over the past five years, and insurance premiums and the cost of penalties. Have there been any such suits filed by staff due to the public's open access to computers in your library?

2. *Automate.* Learning management software (LMS) can track data as courses taken and learners' performance before and after. However, LMS can be pricey, ranging into the mid-six-figure range. Tracking the staff's progress in the e-training environment is a relatively simple function, as long as there is an understanding between the administration and staff that data collected regarding e-training habits will not be used against them.

3. *Maximize training benefits.* Reinforce training benefits through practice and positive reinforcement such as rewards, notes, special honors, and recognition in a library wide e-mail. These measures can stimulate results and amplify training efficiency.

4. *Measure customer satisfaction levels* before *and* after *training.* Through surveys and focus groups with customers, measure their satisfaction with services that can serve as a direct link be-

tween what has been learned by the staff and the means by which it has affected customers. This can be accomplished with the goal of ascertaining whether or not the e-training program has been successful.

5. *Consider the payback period.* For maximum persuasiveness, the ROI report should include the payback time. For example, if the library invests $100,000 the first year in its e-training program, what is the estimated time in terms of staff retention, increased staff recruitment, customer satisfaction, increased usage of library programs and services, and so on, in which the library is likely to see that 200 percent market value returned?

It may be wise for the library to try a small-scale implementation of an e-training program using a control group that includes a representative sample of the staff. This demonstration program will identify the courses to be offered, the outcomes sought and, by the use of pre- and posttesting, other determinant factors in order to determine the success of the program. If the ROI report results prove positive, the library administration would be more likely to roll out the program for the entire staff.

By writing and submitting a *defensible* ROI report on staff training, library managers can improve their chances at securing funding for newer, more advanced learning initiatives. As technology reinvents itself in shorter time spans than ever before, newer technologies will undoubtedly be developed to deliver e-training in a more effective manner to even larger learning audiences.

The ROI report can provide a solid foundation for optimizing training the library is already conducting, thus creating a strong case for its continued existence. As available funding for libraries remains flat or shrinks in the near future, it is likely that ROI will play a larger role in how program decisions are made. More often than not, it will be increasingly difficult to get a non-ROI project approved. Although it is not always easy to quantify, track, capture, calculate, and report every cost and benefit regarding training, if the data are collected and justified, the e-training program will find a level of sustainability in the library.

Chapter 8

Is the Library Continuing Education Program Working? Evaluating the Training Program

In his book *Evaluating Training Programs,* Donald Kirkpatrick, the guru of training evaluation, writes, "The reason for evaluating is to determine the effectiveness of a training program."[1] This simple statement is the key to determining the measurable outcomes of the library training program. It opens a world of strategies that may be utilized in order to evaluate its success. In 1959, Kirkpatrick created what is today the most widely used model for training evaluation. Kirkpatrick identified four levels of training evaluation data:

- *Reactions*—measures what participants think and feel about training
- *Learning*—measures how much the training participants increased their skill and knowledge
- *Behavior*—measures on-the-job behavior of the trainees after the training program, as contrasted to the behavior before the program
- *Results*—measure the impact of training on organizational performance metrics[2]

For purposes of evaluating the staff training program created and implemented for a multitype library consortium, this author has designed several evaluation tools for the library training program and the learning outcomes where not only the effectiveness of the program but also the impact it had on the participants were measured. Samples of two questionnaires may be found in Appendix C of this book.

WHY A QUESTIONNAIRE?

- Questionnaires are very cost effective when compared to face-to-face interviews. This is especially true for studies involving large sample sizes and large geographic areas.
- Questionnaires are easy to analyze.
- Questionnaires are familiar to most people. Nearly everyone has had some experience completing questionnaires and they generally do not make people apprehensive.
- Questionnaires reduce bias. The researcher's own opinions will not influence the respondent to answer questions in a certain manner.
- Questionnaires are less intrusive than telephone or face-to-face surveys. Unlike other research methods, the respondent is not interrupted by the research instrument.[3]

The questionnaires were distributed to those who had taken part in an ongoing library training program and sought to elicit results that proved satisfactory to the managers of the program.

ASTD EVALUATION TOOLS

The American Society for Training and Development (ASTD) has developed a number of tools that may be employed to gather the appropriate information by which to measure the accomplishments of those who have participated in the training program. The reader may freely review the tools that this author has modified, where necessary, in order to reflect the library training environment.

The evaluation tools include the following:

1. The Evaluation Matrix
2. Anecdotal Record Form

3. Expert Review Checklist
4. Focus Group Protocol
5. Formative Review Log
6. Interview Protocol
7. Questionnaire

FAILURES OF EVALUATION

Evaluation of the staff training program does not succeed all of the time. The following are some suggested reasons that companies fail to do training evaluations correctly and thereby fail to get valid business or performance results. The reasons are listed in order of process.

1. Lack of planning
2. Assumption that training is a cost rather than an asset
3. Lack of sponsorship
4. Lack of budget
5. Lack of appropriate resources (such as skilled and experienced people in the area in question)
6. Lack of understanding what is important to measure (results do not match key performance measures)
7. Evaluation techniques that do not capture human performance, only the performance of the trainers and training materials
8. Lack of valid measurements, resulting in false data reports
9. Lack of data collection
10. Lack of data analysis and summary[4]

KEY QUESTIONS TO ASK

The evaluation team must ask several key questions to ascertain how the training program has affected the participants and the library itself. For example,

- Is the training content accurate and relevant to the participants' jobs?
- Is the training information presented well by the instructor?
- Is the training timely (not too early or too late)?
- Did the participants increase their knowledge or skill in the training session?
- Did the participants retain what they learned?
- Are the participants applying what they learned back on the job? If not, why?
- Do the work processes allow the participants to apply what they learned?
- Are there barriers to using the training back on the job?[5]

The Ebbinghaus Forgetting Curve

Perhaps the most important questions the library administrators must ask regarding the success of the library training program are What was retained by the staff on completion of training? and Could what they learned be immediately applied in the library? The library administrator should always maintain the image of the "Ebbinghaus Forgetting Curve" when it comes to staff training. Hermann Ebbinghaus (1850-1909) was the first psychologist to investigate learning and memory experimentally. Given this quantitative treatment, Ebbinghaus's methodological innovations, and the care with which he carried out his research, it is not surprising that his results have stood the test of time. Indeed, in the century since the publication of his monograph, surprisingly little has been learned about rote learning and retention that was not already known to Ebbinghaus.

His work remains the hallmark in the area of experimental psychology. Among many other accomplishments in the furtherance of evaluation and learning theory, Ebbinghaus

- reported that the time required to memorize an average nonsense syllable increases sharply as the number of syllables increases;

- noted that continuing to practice material after the learning criterion has been reached enhances retention—the over-learning effect; and
- practiced a list until he was able to repeat the items correctly twice in a row. He then waited varying lengths of time before testing himself again. Forgetting turned out to occur most rapidly soon after the end of practice, but the rate of forgetting slowed as time went on. This curve represented the first forgetting curve.[6]

Ebbinghaus discovered that people forget 90 percent of what they learn in a class within thirty days. In assessing the retention of lists containing nonsense syllables, he found that a very rapid forgetting occurs within in the first hour (50 percent or more). This forgetting, he discovered, flattened out at about 30 percent for delays of up to two days. Thus, it becomes paramount for participants in the staff training program to apply learned knowledge to their job immediately upon return to the workplace. The value of this to evaluation process is extremely important. In order to obtain reliable evaluation results, staff must be able to evaluate the program under optimal circumstances.

Chapter 9

Library Training:
A Future Perspective

Traditionally, the futurist fulfills a role not as a predictor of what *will* occur but as a data prospector who examines the current environment and, based on the finds uncovered during this prospecting endeavor, presents a plausible scenario for what the future *could* resemble. In a sense, the previous chapters of this book have served as an exercise in prospecting without benefit of an organized and comprehensive wrap-up. It is clear that the state of training in libraries allows for tremendous growth and expansion. Let us take a few steps in seeking a viable framework for the future scenario of library staff training.

OVERCOMING RESISTANCE TO TRAINING

According to futurist Alvin Toffler, a fair number of people react to excessive change by turning to the "unchangeable" past for peace of mind.[1] Such peace of mind is engendered by the individual's apparent ability to transcend the present and live in the past, exhibiting little need to accept the future when change approaches. This individual's comfort level with the past is such that he or she remains fixed and unmoving when asked to attend training that will help to upgrade skills and/or teach something new. Such individuals will reply that they have learned enough and could not possibly learn one more thing, as if, should they actually learn that "one more thing," their entire consciousness would be emptied of all they had previously learned to make room for the new. Of course, this is a ridiculous notion, but one that this author has heard expressed often.

In a short story by Jorge Luis Borges, titled, "Funes the Memorious," the protagonist eventually perishes because he can never forget all that he has learned and every single speck of information fed to him is retained until he finally expires due to, for lack of a better term, information overload. Staff working in libraries using a similar reply when asked to attend training should be directed to read this story.

When asked to attend training, staff may also state that they have spent years, perhaps decades, performing their jobs effectively without the assistance of additional training, technological support, or upgraded skills. Why should they change their work habits now? Similarly, they may say they are still actively engaged in the workplace. They have not been fired, so obviously whatever they are doing has been successful. Likewise, why change *their* work style now? Both of these groups may be performing terribly at their jobs, but they do not feel the need to upgrade their skills or change their habits. What will these people do, or where they will go, when change comes to the library and they have no choice but to adapt or move on? There will be little room for those who have not adapted to the changed environment.

Creating Fun in the Workplace

If the notion of *workplace as learning place* is ever to seriously take hold, the mind-set of such library staffers must inevitably change. This can be facilitated by creating a workplace environment of learning and fun. Futurists Malcolm Menzies and Rolf Jensen have written extensively on the sentiment that the workplace of the future will be a place where employees have fun inside the workplace.[2] That is, along with hard work, a sense of fulfillment, respect for one's fellows, and commitment to one's craft, there must be built into the workplace this notion of "hard fun."[3] This does not infer that employees smack each other over the heads each day when they enter the workplace with, say, foam baseball bats. But, according to Jensen, work will be "edifying, playful, engaging, and will demand commitment."[4]

Today, there are many training programs in which teams of employees are removed from the office environment and encouraged to indulge in such physical team-oriented activities as rope climbing, paintball shooting, tugs-of-war, or other examples of "survival" skills. The employees enjoy a workout and a bit of friendly, sometimes strenuous, but usually competitive fun. Taking part in such activities can help employee morale, and employees often perceive co-workers in an entirely different light. Upon completion of these activities and a return to the workplace, staff frequently discover they have more in common with one another than they suspected. The sense of fun may linger for quite some time, often leading to friendlier relations among staff members. Such understanding can lead to commonality of purpose in terms of reaching the ultimate goals of the organization. Also, such exercises can strengthen an individual's commitment to the organization.

These activities also foster a climate of inclusion. Inclusion cannot be overestimated as a means by which staff will accept change. It will assist them in accepting their inevitable movement into the future goals of the workplace. According to Grant Wardlaw,

> No individual, organization or nation is immune from these forces. A society based on the value derived from knowledge will be characterized by networks, innovation, inclusion and speed. To remain competitive (or to *get* competitive) we must all—individuals, organizations and nations—learn to constantly adjust in the present to create the future.[5]

Although Wardlaw's comments have importance in terms of the "knowledge" society, a society in which we presently find ourselves, it is in the "dream society" of the future that Jensen projects we will discover the notion of "hard fun" inside the workplace.

Using "The Story" of the Library

What is the basis of a future workplace that will be found inside this "dream society"? Jensen projects that, along with the concept of "hard fun," organizations will build and offer a sense of the "stories" behind the products and services they provide. In essence, every organization has a history. From where did the original concept of an organization arise? How was the decision made to offer the organization's product or service? Through advertising and promotion, these stories are told and retold. Often, companies and services delve deep into their pasts to forge a connection with the present by relating a story to prove that their current product or service has not strayed from the original intent or concept. Thus, the library has a long and prestigious past from which it will draw on to tell its story in the future.

Libraries have an extraordinary history reaching back thousands of years. This extremely rich history can certainly be mined to demonstrate connection to the library's present services. Centuries of stories can be attached to the library to showcase current service in light of this history. It still provides information, as did its ancient forebear, the Alexandrian Library; it is also on the cutting edge of new technologies. From this unique position, the library's provision of information as its central service can be easily linked to its past. The library must find and examine the appropriate story to link and promote the library service.

On a more local level, there are many library buildings that have a rich history. These stories may foster a sense of belonging and commitment to the library based on a perhaps unique historical past. For example, many libraries have abundant architectural history, or they have served as an original service in the community in which they reside. The library may have had famous users, or famous members of the staff or board. Writers or artists may have been associated with the library. Important collections may be housed within the library. All of these are strengths that should be drawn upon to support the "story" of the library. The public respects these connections and takes pride in promoting them.

Although the library professional has been accused of sometimes looking in the rearview mirror to create the library's future, in terms of the "story" approach to service, and the promotion of the library itself, this may be one instance where this is not an adverse suggestion.

In order for staff to endorse such a concept, a certain sense of pride must be attached to these stories. As the staff is educated and trained to accept the idea of the workplace as learning place, not only for users but for themselves as well, they will come to understand that the stories of their library can be quite useful in gaining public acceptance of what some still might consider a "quaint" or old-fashioned service. The library must indeed link its story to the future and explain how the provision of its services, although based in the past, will benefit future generations of the community in as technology-rich an environment as one can find.

Due to Internet access from home computers, it has been accepted by a certain segment of today's population that libraries are no longer necessary. The latest statistics point to the opposite. According to the 2002 American Library Association use survey, the number of people supporting library current and future usage is enlightening by the extremely high level of support. It was found that:

- 91 percent of the total respondents believed libraries will exist in the future
- 91 percent believe libraries are changing and dynamic places with a variety of activities for the whole family
- 90 percent believe libraries are places of opportunity for education, self-help and offer free access to all
- 88 percent agreed libraries are unique because you have access to nearly everything on the Web or in print, as well as personal service and assistance in finding it
- 83 percent believe libraries and librarians play an essential role in our democracy and are needed now more than ever[6]

This is hardly a surprise to most current library directors and staff, but it should provide heartening support to administrators preparing strategic plans for their libraries in the future.

ELEMENTS IN PLANNING THE LIBRARY FOR THE FUTURE

Regarding future planning, it is accepted that the speed of information technology development will only continue to increase. The time span between one technology completely fusing into the next has shortened to approximately eighteen months. Therefore, in order to be practical and valuable, a long-range strategic plan that includes a technology plan component for the future should not stretch beyond eighteen months. Although the library may well be ready to upgrade its technology before then, it simply may not have the funding to do so.

Sustainability

The key word to prepare the library for its future is *sustainability*. It is more important to plan with this word in mind than with any other single element. Of course, there are numerous issues affecting libraries that may intrude and derail the strategic plan, including funding, the current political climate, the social atmosphere, legal issues, environmental issues, public issues, staffing issues, etc. However, if one accepts the necessity of sustainability, the strategic plan should always include a number of alternate scenarios; in case of disaster, the library manager will be forced to shift to another plan. A word to the wise—plan for a sustainable future. Taking a list compiled from the words of Australian professor Ian Lowe regarding the creation of a sustainable future for the environment, one may consider comparable measures in creating a sustainable future for libraries including:

- going beyond the short term,
- conserving resources based on the rate of resource depletion,
- measuring the impact of [libraries] on social stability,
- nurturing a cultural richness,
- using resources much more efficiently, and
- creating programs and services that are innovative, efficient, and humane[7]

RETAINING THE LIBRARY STAFF FOR THE FUTURE

In order for the library to be successful in the future, the staffing must remain solid, professional, and as sustainable as any other resource managed by the library. Successful recruitment and retention of staff has been an issue that library managers have dealt with for some time. This author has previously discussed the value of a strong and continuous staff training program as a means by which to recruit and retain staff in times of short staffing.

The Association of Research Libraries (ARL) suggests that libraries need to be "extremely flexible organizations" if they are to be successful in the future. "Careers will have to be re-conceptualized and career development will have to be reinvented."[8] ARL continues by stressing that

> Job flexibility, hiring good people and then designing jobs for them, and reconsidering where and how people do their work are all viable strategies for creating an environment to which professional librarians will be attracted and in which they will stay.[9]

THE FUTURE OF TRAINING LIBRARY STAFF

Once it is ascertained that the library and the library staff will remain in place for the future, the staff training program may be designed for them, a program that will continuously stimulate and excite the staff so they will remain in place to tell their stories and offer their service.

When e-learning came onto the scene, certain circles assumed it would circumvent traditional learning and that everyone would take education and training courses delivered online. E-learning has existed long enough now and there have been more than enough studies done to determine that this did not come to pass. Perhaps no more than 30 percent of staff training programs are being digested through e-learning. The vast majority of staff training is learned through a combination of instructor-led delivery and technology such as satellite delivery, television, desktop streaming media, and even videotapes. Jensen suggests we will never truly escape the instructor-led, traditional classroom version of staff education and training

> because of our need for togetherness; because we learn more, communicate more . . . it will not come to pass that in-person meetings, conferences and learning will entirely be delivered virtually. We would simply miss the interaction, body language and communications options.[10]

The "togetherness" aspect of training fits conceptually with the notion of "stories" delivered by the library. The human aspects of both of these approaches cannot be underestimated. We are talking about a much more personal manner in which to deliver the library's *product*, i.e., information. According to futurist author Anne-Marie Dahl, the workplace should accommodate these combined concepts in order to set the scene for the workplace as learning place, comfort zone, home away from home, or what-have-you.

> The new concept of work requires a lot of flexibility from each employee. A stressed-out, burned-out employee can't fulfill these requirements. The workplace should provide peace and space. Leaders should provide guidelines, rituals, traditions and milestones so the employees can navigate among and with each other in the changeable workplace. Workplaces increasingly are going to provide thoughtfulness, support and aid to both the nearly inseparable spheres of work and family. For only through prioritizing the whole human being can you be sure to get qualified labor in the future—it is going to influence the bottom line![11]

The bottom line for staff learning is the "blended" learning approach. The idea behind blended learning is that instructional designers review a learning program, divide it into modules, and determine the best medium to deliver those modules to the learner.

In offering library staff an array of learning modules delivered through a variety of delivery systems, the learner can access the material in any manner he or she chooses. This approach will greatly expand learning opportunities. The future of library staff learning will be evident in its variety and delivery. In this manner, the library training program can adapt to new technologies and learning styles of adult learners.

Chapter 10

Delivering Blended Learning to Library Staff in Southeast Florida: A Case Study

SOUTHEAST FLORIDA LIBRARY INFORMATION NETWORK (SEFLIN)

Due to rapid technological change and turnover in library staff due to attrition and retirement, continuous training and education must be one of the most important priorities for libraries. To address this need, SEFLIN (Southeast Florida Library Information Network) developed a continuing education and training program for more than 3,000 staff members in 350 locations. The aim of the program is to provide quality training in the areas defined by member libraries: library practices, office-related software, information technology, and management. In creating this training program, SEFLIN was not only committed to staff learning. It also wanted to investigate new and developing technologies and to harness these technologies to create a mix of learning tools to support different learning styles.

The program that began in 2000 included only Web-based technology training: technology courses and information technology reference books delivered over the Web and instructor led technology training, courses taught by technology trainers in professional training facilities throughout southeast Florida. As the program has continued, the organization has investigated and demonstrated an array of technologies to maximize usage and provide increased means for delivering education and training. In seeking additional methods for staff to access courses, workshops, and tutorial offerings it eventually arrived at what is today a continuous education program consisting of a number of blended learning tools, nearly all delivered through technology. Programs offered in the SEFLIN continuing education and training program take into account the individual learning styles of employees, the limitations of library training budgets, challenges of managing time away from the workplace, and the large geographic area occupied by member libraries.

A SCALABLE PROGRAM

Although SEFLIN planned its education and training program for a large consortium, this program is scalable to smaller library systems or even individual libraries. The scalability of a blended learning program is evident in its affordability. This program provides a menu-driven approach that offers staff a variety of training tools. It is an approach that presents flexibility for libraries, which can add or subtract courses from the training menu, creating an individually designed learning program model. This is different from a traditional training program that relies on either permanent staff or hires presenters to train a group of staff in a specific area. Although the Library Services and Technology Act, administered by the State Library of Florida, funded this program, it is designed to eventually be sustainable by the member libraries.

Also, SEFLIN has developed a reporting structure that measures the return on investment of the program, a structure that libraries of any size can employ. For SEFLIN, the program has regularly returned triple its investment for member libraries.

WHY BLENDED LEARNING?

The concept behind blended learning is instructional designers create a learning program, divide it into modules, and determine the best medium to deliver those modules to the learner. SEFLIN has progressed since the program began, and today the various media employed include all of the following:

- Traditional classroom or lab settings, reading assignments
- CD-ROM-based training
- Performance support tools (more than 1,000 of the most popular information technology reference books, available online to all staff)
- Access to the Web
- Teletraining (videos of previously presented workshops and seminars)
- Teleconferences (satellite-delivered workshops and seminars on library issues presented by professionals in the field)
- Stand-alone Web-based training (university-level courses designed for Web-only students on library issues)
- Compressed video
- Streaming media
- Asynchronous Web-based training (complete technology training and library issues courses that may be taken at the convenience of the learner)
- Classroom-based technology-assisted formats (courses and workshops where the presenter uses PowerPoint, "live" Web site assistance, or overhead projector and slides to assist his or her presentation)

Often, a module can be delivered in more than one medium. In offering library staff a variety of learning modules through an assortment of delivery systems, the learner can access the material in any manner he or she chooses.

The various training mediums are designed to complement and enhance one another. One example of this enhancement is the Web-based technology training and instructor-led training offered at professional training facilities. SEFLIN has selected vendors whose instructor-led classes have a similar look, feel, and content as the online courses. When library workers return from instructor-led training, they can reinforce their new skills at their own pace with online courseware.

Upon entering into a full-blown blended learning program using primarily technology to support all aspects of its delivery, it is wise to ensure its success through a number of tasks, roles, and tools. The following list identifies some fundamentals critical to the success of any blended learning project.

1. Educate the potential audience on the fundamentals of blended learning.
2. Determine the actual training need.
3. Define your process and communicate it.
4. Identify key project personnel and define their roles.
5. Perform a comprehensive and realistic needs analysis.
6. Consider unique aspects of interface design and media types and sizes when designing program.
7. Perform a thorough analysis regarding the content of the blended learning and the specific instructional treatments.
8. Define your deliverables.
9. Acquire knowledge of your development tools.
10. Test your application early and often, from both a user and technical perspective.[1]

Following is an overview of some of the major delivery methods in our blended learning program and the benefits of each.

WEB-BASED LEARNING

Two elements have been selected to provide the Web-based learning component of the program. The first comes from libraries themselves. There is a great need for basic library-specific education for working professional librarians who are either new to their positions or are seeking refresher tutorials. Other staff members, from circulation staff to information technology (IT) departments, want to learn the issues and language of library service. A number of libraries have created successful online courses and mounted them on the Web. SEFLIN provides links to these Web-based tutorials and promotes them to library staff.

Second, a vendor with a history of providing Web-based technology training was selected to supply a combination of technology and management training. Three specific online-learning modules were purchased, with access provided to every level of library staff. These modules include office productivity software training, which highlights the most widely used desktop and design software packages; high-end information technology training, which provides training to computer professionals; and a suite of business school management skills tutorials.

The benefits of Web-based training are many. Libraries are able to deliver up-to-the-minute information twenty-four hours-a-day in an asynchronous learning environment. The primary benefit of such an environment is flexibility. Library staff can access a full complement of flexible training at their office, home, or on the road. Web-based training is cost efficient; staff can take as many courses, as often as they need, for one annual fee. Library staff can choose either online instructor-led courses (courses taught by professional technology trainers and available in an asynchronous environment over a period of six to eight weeks) or interactive self-paced courses, and they can take advantage of an extensive online reference library (more than 1,000 of the most popular information technology reference books, available online to all staff). They can also tailor learning modules to appropriate interests, career objectives, job profiles, or core competencies.

Finally, Web-based training provides accurate measurement and evaluation of staff who are registered in the program; this allows management to monitor staff progress and performance. SEFLIN has spent several years developing in-house and consultant-designed surveys and evaluations of various components of the program, as well as the entire program itself, in order to study the data received on modes of learning and its effects upon the individual and the library.

INSTRUCTOR-LED E-LEARNING

Instructor-led e-learning involves an in-person instructor teaching a synchronous class of approximately twelve students, all of whom are seated at computer terminals in a professionally equipped training facility. The vendor was selected for its ability to offer training in many professional training facilities throughout Southeast Florida.

The key benefit of this delivery method is flexibility in scheduling training sessions, especially in periods of short staffing. Flexibility in this sense relies upon both the time the course is available and its location. When an individual registers for a course, it is assumed that he or she will be out of the library for an entire day. Courses are scheduled up to two months in advance, thus allowing the library more than enough time to find coverage for the day he or she attends training. If the individual must return to the library after training, he or she can return from the training facility located reasonably close to the library. The staff member takes the course at a professionally equipped facility nearest to his or her work site or home. The courseware used in the training facility is complementary to that being offered through the online vendor. The SEFLIN contract allows staff to repeat the same course at no additional cost.

TELECONFERENCES

Increasingly, workshops and forums are being delivered via satellite, typically called teleconferences. These are being offered by colleges and universities as well as professional and training organizations. SEFLIN has a number of community college members with satellite technology, and teleconferences may be scheduled simultaneously at each of these institutions, allowing staff to attend the site closest to them. Teleconferences are beneficial because they offer training to a large group of staff concurrently, at multiple locations, providing large group training at a minimal cost.

COMPRESSED VIDEO

Interactive compressed video systems allow for two-way video-conferencing between sites. This method of delivery utilizes video cameras and sound in multiple locations. The data are carried over a telephone line and the local telecom provider must coordinate the meeting time and locations. A presenter, or presenters, may be situated in several locations, with the audience in various locations as well. Since the system is interactive, it provides for questions and answers in real time. There are a number of advantages to this style of interactive videoconferencing. It establishes a visual connection among participants. Since a speaker can see and hear remote learners in real time, he or she can use conversation and body language to enhance communication. Frequent interaction increases understanding and encourages more personalized in-struction. Interactive learning strategies such as questioning and discussion can also engage and motivate learners by making them active participants. Perhaps the type of workshop that best lends it-self to this method is an individual lecturer speaking to a group. With the proper equipment in place, the lecturer's camera remains on him or her and the audience camera will follow the voice, thus providing an additional level of personalization to a rather imper-sonal training method.

Compressed video enables connection with external resources. Remote experts can be brought into the program to validate under-standing, provide feedback, and introduce practical examples. This real-world connection can greatly improve motivation, espe-cially if staff participates and the expert interacts at an appropriate level.

Compressed video also supports the use of diverse media. Photos and color graphics look great on video and can help convey a difficult concept or simplify instructions. Room-based systems usually include an attachable document camera that allows trans-mission of high-quality still images. This feature can be used to show objects as well as photos and graphics, and many instructors also project "slates," or simple text displays with a few sentences (usually instructions). Slates are an easy way to shift learner fo-cus from the video screen to a learning activity. Some systems support application sharing, allowing users at each site to see and edit a document. This kind of sharing encourages collaboration and real-time feedback.

STREAMING MEDIA

Streaming media broadcasts video, sound, and text to the desktop computer. As more conference presentations and forums are recorded in remote locations and offered through this mode of delivery, it offers staff the ability to see and hear the latest on library issues without having to attend the original event. There are technical challenges when using this method, not the least of which is the ability of the user's library computer to receive broadband presentations. As more libraries upgrade their telecom connections to T1 or even T3 high-speed lines, this method of training will undoubtedly become more popular. Currently, the software available to create content by using this method is very expensive, but as the price decreases the flexibility of offering video, audio, text, PowerPoint slides, and e-mail capability on the same screen will find a larger audience.

Webcasts allow the individual to participate in a live event by logging in at his or her desktop. The major challenge facing this mode of delivery is the technical capability of the computer to access them. A specific multimedia "plug-in" (a small program or module with the purpose of extending the capabilities of a software application) such as Shockwave, RealPlayer, or Windows Media is required, along with enough bandwidth to accommodate video, audio, and text all at once. SEFLIN is only beginning to use this training method.

CLASSROOM-BASED
TECHNOLOGY-ASSISTED FORMATS

Many adult learners still prefer the traditional form of learning in which instructors stand at the front of the classroom using "live" Internet links, PowerPoint slides, or an overhead projector to support their discussions. These days, it is a rare classroom scenario in which the presenter does not include some technology-based support tool to assist in the presentation. Evaluation surveys indicate that nearly 70 percent of instructor-led workshops and seminars sponsored by SEFLIN include some aspect of technology. SEFLIN has found that content presented in the traditional format is a less technical and more formal method of training; a single speaker using technology assistance (PowerPoint, "live" Web sites, or overhead projector and slides) on library issues still seems to be most popular.

THE FUTURE OF TECHNOLOGY-BASED TRAINING

Annual surveys, evaluations, and focus groups are integral in the selection of materials and the methods of delivery in the training program. Content and quality of the service deliverables are always under review. A blended learning program must offer training materials that are of the highest quality since poor content or faulty delivery in one module can tarnish the entire program. Again, an advantage to blended learning is flexibility. Modules that do not fulfill expectations can be easily replaced.

As the library profession moves forward, library staff education and training needs to be nimble, fluid, and adaptable to new technologies and delivery systems. According to author Judith M. Smith,

> technology is going to be one of the major venues through which people will be learning in the future. This translates to how an [organization] builds and reinforces its members' professional needs as our society evolves into a knowledge management economy. People need survival skills to interact within the culture and society, in addition to the core needs. Training and education that involves technology (note—the word is "involves," meaning includes—but not to the exclusion of all other kinds of learning) will need to be flexible as far as when and where it is taught, and the methods used. Blended learning offers that kind of flexibility.[2]

Appendix A

ROI Courses Offered at U.S. Business Schools

For those who are not yet experienced in producing the ROI report, training courses are offered through a number of prestigious business schools. Such courses may be found listed under *financial engineering, computational finance, mathematics of finance, financial and industrial mathematics,* or *quantitative and computational finance.*

- Boston University School of Management: <http://management.bu.edu>
- Carnegie Mellon University: <http://web.gsia.cmu.edu/default.aspx?id=141030>
- MIT's Sloan School of Management: <http://mitsloan.mit.edu/roi/main.html>

These universities offer similar project management programs:

- Columbia University: <http://www.math.columbia.edu/department/masters_finance.shtml>
- Georgia Institute of Technology: <http://www.math.gatech.edu/academic/graduate/degreeprograms.html>
- Oregon Graduate Institute: <http://cse.ogi.edu/compfin>
- Purdue University: <http://www.stat.purdue.edu/purduecf>
- University of California, Berkeley: <http://haas.berkeley.edu/Phd/finance.html>
- University of Michigan: <http://interpro.engin.umich.edu/fep>

Appendix B

Train-the-Trainer Degrees, Certificates, Workshops, and Courses

Boise State University—Master of Science in Instructional and Performance Technology (on campus, online, or combination of two)

Capella University—Certificate in Training

Claremont University, Claremont, CA—Human Resources Design

Distance Education Clearinghouse—Distance education related certificate programs

Dr. Ruth Clark, Clark Training & Consulting—Instructional Systems Design (ISD) certification program and various training and certification programs

The Fielding Graduate Institute—Human and Organization Development (PhD)

Friesen, Kaye and Associates—Various workshop programs for trainers (performance gap specialists)

Georgetown University—Training Certificate Program

George Washington University—Master of Arts in Educational Technology Leadership (via distance education)

Indiana College Network—Adult education and learning courses (via distance education)

Langevin Learning Services—Train the Trainer workshops and certification programs

North Carolina State University—Various education programs and courses (distance education)

OnlineLearning.Net—Various online courses in Education

Penn State Harrisburg—Master of Education program in Training and Development

Rochester Institute of Technology—Human Resource Management (online)

San Diego—EDTECH—Certificate in Instructional Technology (on-line)

St. John Fisher College—Human Resource Development Degree

Susan Boyd Associates—Train the trainer workshops

TLC Seminars—Presentation Skills, Basic Instructor, and Advance Instructor training programs

The Training Clinic—Train the trainer programs and certificates

University California, Santa Cruz Extension—Certificate in Training and Human Resource Development

University of Colorado—Designing and Implementing Web-based Learning Environments (online)

University of North Texas—Master of Science in Applied Technology, Training and Development (also offers a Corporate Training Certificate)

Webster University—MA degree in Human Resource Development

Appendix C

Staff Training Outcomes Survey Questionnaire

TEMPLATE 1

- This survey is intended to measure your assessment of the training program for library staff.
- Key survey objectives appear in italics above each set of questions to refer to as you reply.
- The information that you provide will directly impact how this library plans future technology training, so please respond responsibly and honestly.
- We ask that you return this survey by_____.
- Thank you very much for your important input, interest, and participation in this program.

Part I: Background

1. What is your position? (Check only one answer.)

   _____ Administration (Director, Assistant Director, Department/Unit Head)

   _____ Public Services (Reference, Circulation, etc.)

   _____ Technical Services (Cataloging, Collection Development, etc.)

   _____ Other Services (Personnel, Accounting, etc.)

2. Does your position require an MLS degree? (Check only one answer.)

   _____ Yes

   _____ No

3. What is your library type? (Check only one answer.)

    _____   Public
    _____   Academic
    _____   Special
    _____   School

4. How many years have you worked in libraries? (Check only one answer.)

    _____   Less than 1 year
    _____   1 to 5 years
    _____   6 to 10 years
    _____   11 to 15 years
    _____   16 to 20 years
    _____   More than 20 years

5. What type of classes/courses have you taken? (Check all categories that apply.)

    _____   Instructor-led (Web)
    _____   Self Study (Web)
    _____   Instructor-led (face to face)
    _____   Teleconference

Part II: Knowledge/Skills in Using Technology

Scale for Answering Questions in Part II

Please select the number that applies to each question and write it in the provided space.

Not at all	1
Rarely	2
To a moderate extent	3
To a great extent	4
To a very great extent	5

Use of Technology Knowledge/Skills Before and After Training

   _____   6. To what extent did you use technology knowledge/skills *before* taking classes through the library technology training program?

   _____   7. To what extent are you using technology knowledge/skills *after* taking classes through the library technology training program?

Confidence in Ability to Use Technology Knowledge/Skills

   _____   8. To what extent has your confidence in using technology increased as a result of the library technology training program?

Support and Barriers to Learning

   _____   9. To what extent did you receive assistance from your local library training administrator in preparing you for the library training program?

   _____   10. To what extent have you received help and/or support from your direct supervisor in applying the technology knowledge/skills learned through the library training program?

   _____   11. To what extent have you used the technology knowledge/skills learned through the library technology training program?

   _____   12. To what extent have you had access to the necessary resources (e.g., equipment and information) to apply the technology knowledge/skills learned in the library technology training program?

Learning Impact Measures

   _____   13. To what extent has the content of courses taken through the library training program accurately reflected the technology knowledge/skills needed on your job?

   _____   14. To what extent has the library training program improved your *daily* performance on the job?

   _____   15. To what extent has the library training program improved your *overall* job performance?

Part III: Program Design and Delivery

Scale for Answering Questions in Part III

Please select the number that applies to each question and write it in the provided space. (Note the different rating indicators in this scale.)

Strongly Disagree	1
Disagree	2
Neither	3
Agree	4
Strongly Agree	5

Effectiveness of Delivery Methods

_____ 16. Live instructor-led classes held in library technology training labs are an effective way to learn.

_____ 17. Teleconference (or other technology-delivered) classes held in CompUSA training labs are an effective way to learn.

_____ 18. Web-based courses delivered online are an effective way to learn.

19. Training facilities and equipment were favorable to learning:
_____ At library technology training labs
_____ At vendor training labs
_____ At your local library job site
_____ At your home

_____ 20. I was able to take technology classes/courses at a time and place convenient for my schedule.

Content

_____ 21. I had the information needed to start each class/course.
_____ 22. I clearly understood class/course objectives.
_____ 23. Classes/courses met all stated objectives.
24. If you have taken instructor-led classes:
_____ Materials provided were useful
_____ I had enough time to learn the subject matter

_____ Course/class content was logically organized
_____ Help was available when I needed assistance

25. If you have taken Web-based courses online:
    _____ Materials provided were useful
    _____ I had enough time to learn the subject matter
    _____ Course/class content was logically organized
    _____ Help was available when I needed assistance

Rating of Program Design and Delivery

26. How would you rate the overall program design and delivery of the library training program? (Check only one answer.)
    _____ Excellent
    _____ Good
    _____ Average
    _____ Below Average
    _____ Failure

Improving Program Design and Delivery

27. What is your single most important recommendation for improving the *quality of instruction* in the library training program?

28. What are your specific or general recommendations for making the library training program better address your needs?

Part IV: Impact of Learned Knowledge/Skills on Library Users

29. The ultimate goal of the library training program is to improve library services for library users. Do you have a specific experience you can share on how a library user(s) has been better served or a library service improved due to your new technology knowledge/skills? Please share as

much detail as appropriate. If you prefer, please attach your written story to the survey.

30. Other comments

TEMPLATE 2

This template is designed to elicit specific information regarding outcomes of a library training program and may be administered to the managers of the program.

1. Which best describes the library which you work in or manage? (Select only one.)

   _____   College or university library
   _____   Community college library
   _____   Public library or public library system
   _____   School district library

2. What is your primary job role? (Select only one.)

   _____   Administration services librarian
   _____   Analyst (creating reports, analyzing data, making recommendations, etc.)
   _____   Children/youth services librarian
   _____   Document specialist
   _____   Reference librarian
   _____   Reference services librarian
   _____   Researcher/information specialist (performing primary or secondary research)
   _____   Serials librarian
   _____   Subject specialist
   _____   Systems librarian/analyst
   _____   Technical services librarian/cataloger
   _____   Training consultant/user education specialist
   _____   Web site developer/knowledge architect or integrator/taxonomy specialist

3. What methods are available to users for interacting with your library services? (Select all that apply.)

_____ Chat room service
_____ Cobrowsing
_____ E-mail
_____ Escorting users to Web sites
_____ Fax
_____ Global telephone number
_____ Live assistance with database searching, tutorials, etc.
_____ Local telephone number
_____ Pushing Web pages
_____ Real-time videoconferencing
_____ Searchable FAQs database
_____ Virtual reference desk software
_____ Walk-in
_____ Web forms
_____ Other, specify: _____

4. What is the average number of training hours *each* of your library's employees receives in a year? Do you think this number will increase or decrease in the coming year _____

5. What, if any, system(s) or process(es) do you have in place to stimulate staff participation in the library training program? (Check all that apply.)
_____ In-kind rewards, e.g., merchandise
_____ Monetary rewards apart from planned compensation (salary, bonus, etc.)
_____ Monetary, but as part of performance management and planned compensation
_____ Recognition at department/division or library- or institution-wide events
_____ Support for annual permanence review
_____ Support for promotion/or rank
_____ Time-off awards

6. What department or division is in charge of the continuing and training initiative and provides leadership and direction in your library? (Select all that apply.)
_____ Administrative
_____ Executive management
_____ Faculty

_____ Human resources
_____ Information center, information resources
_____ Knowledge/information management
_____ Members of general public
_____ New staff orientation
_____ Strategic or program planning
_____ Training administration
_____ Other, specify:
_____ Not applicable

7. How would you like to see your library deploy continuing education and training to staff working in your library in the future? Please indicate percentages of each below. (Your responses should add up to 100 percent.)
_____ Cable TV, satellite TV
_____ Diskette
_____ DVD
_____ E-mail
_____ Fax
_____ In person (including classroom, telephone, voicemail)
_____ Intranet
_____ Open Internet or Portal
_____ Print
_____ Proprietary software or application
_____ Tape (audio, magnetic, video)
_____ Wireless
_____ Other, specify:
_____ Don't know

8. Do you have a dedicated resource(s) to ensure that knowledge gained through the library training program is shared among individuals in your library? (Select all that apply.)
_____ Core competencies requirement fulfillment
_____ Department meetings
_____ Intranet education and training page
_____ One-on-one (staff-to-staff) training program
_____ Other, specify:
_____ Train-the-trainer program

9. From the following list, please indicate which best describes the level of library support your library has designated for the library training program. (Select all that apply.)

    _____   A part-time dedicated person within my library

    _____   A full-time dedicated person within my library

    _____   A dedicated person outside my library

    _____   Support distributed across members of the library staff

    _____   No support, is managed by the head of the library as time permits

    _____   No support at all

    _____   Don't know

10. What would be the three most helpful components to you on a library training Web site?

    a.

    b.

    c.

11. Thinking of all the services you offer and manage, what are the top three issues or challenges your library is currently facing?

    a.

    b.

    c.

12. a. Can the library training program provide assistance and solutions to these issues or challenges?

    _____   Yes

    _____   No

    b. If yes, in your opinion, how best can this be accomplished?

Appendix D

A Sample User Survey for Online Learning

The use of Web-based learning tools continues to meet or in some cases exceed expectations. In this short survey, the instructional designers seek responses so that they may examine the Web-based component of a blended learning program for libraries. Please check the box or boxes next to the appropriate selection(s).

1. How often each week do you access Web-based learning tools? (Check one)
   ☐ Less than once
   ☐ Once or twice
   ☐ Twice or three times
   ☐ More than three times
2. Where do you log on to a computer to access Web-based learning tools? (Check one)
   ☐ At work
   ☐ At home
   ☐ Both work and home
3. Do you have a place (e.g., office) to access Web-based learning tools that is relatively free from interruptions?
   ☐ Yes
   ☐ No
4. What is your *primary* reason for accessing Web-based learning tools? (Check one)
   ☐ The subject interests me
   ☐ My library requires me to take classes
   ☐ I enjoy distance learning
   ☐ I use it mainly for reference

5. As a student accessing Web-based learning tools, which *one* of the following characteristics do you see in yourself ?
   ☐ Self-motivated
   ☐ Disciplined
   ☐ Independent
   ☐ Easily discouraged
6. Do you like the idea of learning on your own?
   ☐ Yes
   ☐ No
7. How would you classify your time management skills? (Check one)
   ☐ Excellent
   ☐ Very good
   ☐ Good
   ☐ Fair
   ☐ Poor
8. What is your comfort level with computers? (Check one)
   ☐ Very comfortable
   ☐ Somewhat comfortable
   ☐ Not comfortable
9. Have you accessed Web-based learning tools that are: (Check all that apply.)
   ☐ Self-study
   ☐ Instructor led
   ☐ Self-study and instructor led
10. Will you access Web-based learning tools in the future?
    ☐ Yes
    ☐ No
11. Do you feel Web-based learning tools have positively impacted your job performance and delivery of service?
    ☐ Yes
    ☐ No

Appendix E

A Sample Needs Assessment Survey for Blended Learning

We ask that you take a moment to participate in this survey. We are seeking to prepare a program of blended learning opportunities for staff working in the library. The definition of blended learning is learning in which you participate in using a variety of methods. We wish to design our program for the upcoming year with your direct input to provide the subject areas and the delivery methods most requested by staff. We appreciate your attention to this survey. Your opinions are extremely important to us.

1. What method(s) would you *most prefer* to participate in the library blended learning program? (Check all that apply to you.)

    ☐ Web-based technology learning (through an online learning provider)

    ☐ Web-based library-specific learning (on a library-related issue)

    ☐ Instructor-led technology learning (at a professional technology training facility)

    ☐ Instructor-led technology-assisted learning (instructor using a PowerPoint presentation or an overhead projector)

    ☐ Attend a teleconference

    ☐ Borrowing and viewing a VHS learning video

    ☐ Viewing or listening to a streaming media lecture or tutorial on my computer

2. Are there particular times of the day that are better for you to participate in library continuing education classes, workshops, or tutorials?

    ☐ No

    ☐ Yes. If yes, please list those times of the day. _____

_____

_____

3. I am interested in attending library training/workshops held *in my library* for career advancement or professional enhancement.
   ☐ No
   ☐ Yes. If yes, please suggest topics of interest. _____

   _____

   _____

   _____

4. I am interested in attending *off-site* library training/workshops for career advancement or professional enhancement.
   ☐ No
   ☐ Yes. If yes, please suggest topics of interest. _____

   _____

   _____

   _____

5. While at work in my library, I have access to a personal computer.
   ☐ No
   ☐ Yes

6. I would like further training in computer skills.
   ☐ No
   ☐ Yes. If yes, list those skills._____

   _____

   _____

   _____

7. Are there problems that will make it difficult to participate in the library continuing education classes, workshops, or tutorials?
   ☐ No
   ☐ Yes. If yes, please list those problems. _____

   _____

   _____

   _____

8. What staff development or training sessions would be most helpful for you in the coming year? _____

   _____

9. My job title is:
   ☐ Administrator
   ☐ Librarian
   ☐ Library assistant
   ☐ Support (clerical)
   ☐ Information technology (or systems)
   ☐ Public relations
   ☐ Accountant
   ☐ Graduate intern

Notes

Chapter 1

1. Easterly, William (2001). *The Elusive Quest for Growth.* Cambridge, MA: The MIT Press, p. 47.

2. Friess, Steve (2002). "Libraries Enjoying Increase in Building, Visitors." *USA Today,* June 19. Retrieved from the Web site: <http://www.usatoday.com/news/education/2002=06=20=libraries.htm>, November 19, 2003.

3. Wiley, Carolyn (1997). "Employee Turnover: Analyzing Employee Movement Out of the Organization." In Frank J. Ofsanko and Nancy K. Napier (Eds.), *Effective Human Resource Measurement Techniques: A Handbook for Practitioners,* Second Edition (pp. 52-60). Alexandria, VA: Society for Human Resource Management, p. 52.

4. Van Buren, Mark E. and Erskine, William (2002). *State of the Industry Report 2002.* Alexandria, VA: ASTD.

5. Galvin, Tammy (2003). "The 2003 Training Top 100." *Training,* March, p. 40.

Chapter 2

1. Ad Hoc Task Force on Recruitment & Retention Issues (2002). "Recruitment, Retention and Restructuring: Human Resources in Academic Libraries." Available online at <http://www.ala.org/ala/acrl/acrlissues/acrlrecruiting/recruitingprofession.htm>.

2. Ibid.

3. Ibid.

4. Lynch, Mary Jo (2002). "Reaching 65." *American Libraries,* March, p. 55.

5. Retrieved from the Web site, May 20, 2003. Available online at <http://www.imls.gov/whatsnew/current/020303.htm>.

6. Kaufman, Paula T. (2002). "Where Do the Next 'We' Come from? Recruiting, Retaining, and Developing Our Successors." *ARL Bimonthly Report,* 221, April. Retrieved from the Web site: <http://www.art.org/newsltr/221/recruit.html>, November 17, 2003.

7. Bridges, William (1994). "The End of the Job." *Fortune* 130(6): 71.

8. Retrieved from the SEFLIN Web site, May 12, 2003. Available online at <http://www.seflin.org/sunseek/what.1.cfm>.

9. Ibid.

Chapter 3

1. Bassi, Laurie J., Ludwig, Jens, McMurrer, Daniel P., and Van Buren, Mark (2000). "Profiting from Learning: Do Firms' Investments in Education and Training Pay Off?" Available online at <http://www.astd.org/virtual_community/research/PFLWhitePaper.pdf>.

Chapter 4

1. Ziegler, Richard (2002). "Hop On Up Here." *Training and Development,* June, p. 21.

2. Hofmann, Jennifer (2001). "Blended Learning Case Study." *Learning Circuits,* April. Available online at <http://www.learningcircuits.org/2001/apr 2001/hofmann.html>.

3. American Society for Training and Development (2002). *State of the Industry: ASTD's Annual Review of Trends in Employer-Provided Training in the United States* (Executive Summary). Alexandria, VA: American Society for Training and Development, p. 2.

4. Ibid, p. 4.

5. Anderson, Terri (2002). "Is E-Learning Right for Your Organization?" *Learning Circuits,* January. Available online at <http://www.learningcircuits. org/2002/jan2002/anderson.html>.

6. American Society for Training and Development (2002). *State of the Industry: ASTD's Annual Review of Trends in Employer-Provided Training in the United States* (Executive Summary). Alexandria, VA: ASTD.

Chapter 5

1. Deming, Basil (2001). "Ten Steps to Being Positively Engaging." *Training and Development,* January, pp. 18-19.

Chapter 6

1. Schroll, Craig (2002). "Conference Attendance Improves Knowledge & Skills." Available online at <http://hazard.com/library/confer.html>.

2. Ibid.

3. Kilian, Claire M. and Hukai, Dawn (2002). "Conference Island." *Training and Development,* 56(4): 19-21.

4. "Education and Continuous Learning" (2000). *ALAAction* No. 3 in a series. May 10. Available online at <http://www.ala.org/ala/ourassociation/governingdocs/keyactionareas/educationaction/educationcontinuing.htm>.

5. "Why Certification?" Oklahoma Certification Manual for Public Librarians. Available online at <http://www.odl.state.ok.us/servlibs/certman/certwhy.htm>.

Chapter 7

1. Phillips, Patti P. Retrieved from the Web site, May 20, 2003. Available online at <http://roi.astd.org/tools_and_resources/Whitepaper.pdf>.

Chapter 8

1. Kirkpatrick, Donald L. (1998). *Evaluating Training Programs,* Second Edition. San Francisco: Berrett-Koehler Publishers, Inc, p. 3.
2. Long, Larry N. (1999). "ROI: Capturing the Big Picture." *Technical Training,* November/December, p. 32.
3. Statpac, Inc. (2003). "Advantages of Written Questionnaires." Available online at <http://www.statpac.com/surveys/advantages.htm>.
4. Abernathy, Donna J. (2001). "Thinking Outside the Evaluation Box." PDF download available for purchase at Amazon.com.
5. Long, "ROI," p. 32.
6. "A Pioneer of the Scientific Study of Memory: Hermann Ebbinghaus." Available online at <www.ssc.uwo.ca/psychology/undergraduate/psych338b/ppt_2003/338B_2003_1.ppt>.

Chapter 9

1. Toffler, Alvin (1970). *Future Shock.* New York: Random House.
2. Menzies, Malcolm (1997). "Leading and Managing in the 21st Century." *Future Times Journal,* Vol. 2.
3. Jensen, Rolf (1999). *The Dream Society.* New York: McGraw-Hill, p. 115.
4. Ibid, p. 116.
5. Wardlaw, Grant (2000). "Pathways to the Knowledge Society: The Role of Futures Thinking." *E-Future Times,* 3(November): 3.
6. "Public Library Use" (ALA Library Fact Sheet Number 6). Available online at <http://www.ala.org/library/fact6.html>.
7. Coote, Jennifer (2001). "Shaping a Sustainable Future—The Need for Fundamental Change." *E-Future Times,* 4(March): 2.
8. Kaufman, Paula T. (2002). "Where Do the Next 'We' Come From? Recruting, Retaining and Developing Our Successors. *ARL Monthly Report,* 221(April): 4.
9. Ibid.
10. Jensen, *The Dream Society,* p. 68.
11. Dahl, Anne-Marie. "Work and Family in the Future—A Struggle for Time?" Available online at <http://www.cifs.dk>.

Chapter 10

1. Steiner, Mark. "The Top 10 Strategies for a Successful E-Learning Project." Available online at <http://www1.astd.org/tk03/interact/pdfs/MSteiner.pdf>.

2. Smith, Judith M. "Blended Learning: An Old Friend Gets a New Name." *Executive Update Online.* Available online at <http://www.gwsae.org/Executiveupdate/2001/March/blended.htm>.

Selected Training Bibliographies

There are, quite literally, tens of thousands of reference resources in the area of corporate training and development. More are being written every year. Therefore, I have chosen to include those that, although not specifically written for the library community, I consider pertinent to support much of the subject matter examined in this book. In my book, *The Practical Library Manager* (The Haworth Press, 2003), the reader can find a bibliography of training references selected specifically from library literature. Materials selected for the following bibliographies emphasize that training can cross the corporate line into the world of libraries with great ease. The commonalities and similarities of issues involved in training are not, in the least, unique to the corporate environment.

LEADERSHIP DEVELOPMENT

Alldredge, Margaret E. and Nilan, Kevin J. (2000). "3M's leadership competency model: An internally developed solution." *Human Resource Management,* 39(2/3): 133-145.

Allerton, Haidee (2000). "Leadership A to Z." *Training & Development,* 54(3): 58-61.

Anonymous (2000). "Bayer's leadership training transcends division boundaries." *The New Corporate University Review,* 8(2): 17.

Arthur, Jodi Spiegel (2000). "Staying on top." *Human Resource Executive,* 14(7): 65-68.

Barnett, Carole K. and Tichy, Noel M. (2000). "Rapid cycle CEO development: How new leaders learn to take charge." *Organizational Dynamics,* 29(1): 16-32.

Bossidy, Larry (2001). "The job no CEO should delegate." *Harvard Business Review,* 79(3): 46-49.

Bruzzese, Anita (2000). "Blazing the trail." *Human Resource Executive,* 14(7): 70-72.

Buss, Dale (2001). "When managing isn't enough: Nine ways to develop the leaders you need." *Workforce,* 80(12): 44-48.

Caudron, Shari (2000). "Building better bosses." *Workforce,* 79(5): 32-39.

Conner, Jill (2000). "Developing the global leaders of tomorrow." *Human Resource Management,* 39(2/3): 147-157.

Daniels, Cora (2000). "This man wants to help you. Seriously." *Fortune,* 142(1): 327-330.

Delahoussaye, Martin (2002). "Licking the leadership crisis." *Training,* 39(1): 24-29.

Delahoussaye, Martin (2002). "When tomorrow comes." *Training,* 39(3): 32-36.

Friedman, Stewart D. (2001). "Leadership DNA: The Ford Motor story." *Training and Development,* 55(3): 22-29.

Fulmer, Robert M., Gibbs, Philip A., and Goldsmith, Marshall (2000). "Developing leaders: How winning companies keep on winning." *Sloan Management Review,* 42(1): 49-59.

Fulmer, Robert M. and Goldsmith, Marshall (2001). *The leadership investment.* New York: AMACOM.

Fulmer, Robert M. and Wagner, Stacey (1999). "Leadership: Lessons from the best." *Training & Development,* 53(3): 28-32.

Gale, Sarah Fister (2001). "Bringing good leaders to light." *Training,* 38(6): 38-42.

Geber, Beverly (2000). "Who will replace those vanishing execs?" *Training,* 37(7): 48-53.

Goldwasser, Donna (2001). "Reinventing the wheel." *Training,* 38(2): 54-65.

Hammonds, Keith H. (2000). "Grassroots leadership." *Fast Company,* 33: 138-152.

Lawler, William (2000). "The consortium approach to grooming future leaders." *Training & Development,* 54(3): 53-57.

Lombardo, Michael M. and Eichinger, Robert W. (2000). "High potential as high learners." *Human Resource Management,* 39(4): 321-329.

McDermott, Lynda C. (2001). "Developing the new young managers." *Training & Development,* 55(10): 42-48.

Meryer, Tom (2001). "Ten tips for leadership trainers." *Training & Development,* 55(3): 16-17.

Mulligan, Deborah R. (2001). *In action: Creating mentoring and coaching programs.* Alexandria, VA: ASTD.

Neary, D. Bradford and O'Grady, Don A. (2000). "The role of training in developing global leaders: A case study at TRW Inc." *Human Resource Management,* 39(2): 185-193.

Patton, Carol (2000). "The middle way." *Human Resource Executive,* 14(10): 84-85.

Phillips, Jack J. (Ed.) (1999). *In action: Effective leadership programs.* Alexandria, VA: ASTD.

Pulley, Mary Lynn, Sessa, Valerie, and Malloy, Michelle (2002). "E-leadership: A two-pronged idea." *Training & Development,* 56(3): 34-47.

Recardo, Ronald J. (2000). "Best practices in organizations experiencing extensive and rapid change." *National Productivity Review,* 19(3): 79-85.

Rhodes, Kale (2002). "Breaking in the top dogs." *Training,* 37(2): 66-74.

Tarley, Marshall (2002). "Leadership development for small organizations." *Training & Development,* 56(3): 52-55.

Weiss, Ruth Palombo (2002). "Crisis leadership." *Training & Development,* 56(3): 28-33.

Wellins, Richard and Byham,William (2001). "Where have all the leaders gone? The leadership gap." *Training,* 38(3): 98-106.

Yearout, Steve, Miles, Gerry, and Koonce, Richard (2000). "Wanted: Leader-builders." *Training & Development,* 54(3): 34-42.

Zenger, Jack, Ulrich, Dave, and Smallwood, Norm (2000). "The new leadership development." *Training & Development,* 54(3): 22-27.

TRAINING BUDGETS

Allerton, Haidee (1996). "What things cost." *Training & Development,* 50(6): 20-23.

Anonymous (1997). "To centralize or not to centralize your budget." *Training Directors' Forum Newsletter,* 13(3): 5.

Anonymous (2000). "Six rules for running training like a business—Part I." *The New Corporate University Review,* 8(2): 5-7.

Anonymous (2000). "Six rules for running training like a business—Part II." *The New Corporate University Review,* 8(3): 16-17.

Anonymous (2000). "The money." *Training,* 37(10): 51-55.

Densford, Lynn E. (1998). "Sun Microsystems: Finding new ways to put training in context." *Corporate University Review,* 6(6): 20-22.

Flynn, Gillian (1998). "Training budgets 101." *Workforce,* 77(11): 91-92.

Galvin, Tammy (2001). "Top 50 training organizations: Birds of a feather." *Training,* 38(3): 57-88.

Kasten, Paul (1998). "Customer service training: Within budget." *Technical Training,* 9(1): 20-22.

Kuhn, Nancy (1998). "Training from scratch." *Training & Development,* 52(10): 44-49.

Miner, Nanette (2001). "The one-person training department [Booklet]." Alexandria, VA: ASTD, INFO-LINE.

Nilson, Carolyn (1999). *How to start a training program: Training is a strategic business tool in any organization,* Alexandria, VA: ASTD.

Schriver, Rob and Giles, Steve (1998). "Where have all the $$$ gone?" *Technical Training,* 9(4): 22-25.

Waagen, Alice K. (2000). "How to budget training" [Booklet]. Alexandria, VA: ASTD.

VALUE OF TRAINING

Anonymous (2000). "Employers maximize development to minimize turnover." *Workforce Strategies,* 18(4): WS19-WS21.

Bassi, Laurie J. and McMurrer, Daniel P. (1998). "Training investment can mean financial performance." *Training & Development,* 52(5): 40-42.

Benabou, Charles (1996). "Assessing the impact of training programs on the bottom line." *National Productivity Review,* 15(3): 91-99.

Bernstein, David S. (1999). "Satisfaction guaranteed?" *Inside Technology Training,* 3(4): 12-15, 58.

Crouch, Nigel (1997). "Winning ways." *People Management,* 3(19): 40-42.

Dobbs, Kevin (1999). "Winning the retention game." *Training,* 36(9): 50-56.

Herman, Roger E. (1999). "Stability is watchword for effective workforce." *HRFocus,* 76(6): S1-S3.

Lachnit, Carroll (2001). "Training proves its worth." *Workforce,* 80(9): 52-56.

Lyau, Nyan-Myau and Pucel, David J. (1995). "Economic return on training investment at the organization level." *Performance Improvement Quarterly,* 8(3): 68-79.

Olesen, Margaret (1999). "What makes employees stay." *Training & Development,* 53(10): 48-52.

Reingold, Jennifer and McNatt, Robert (1999). "Why Your Workers Might Jump Ship." *Business Week,* 3618 (March 1): 8.

West, Michael and Patterson, Malcolm (1998). "Profitable personnel." *People Management,* 4(1): 28-31.

Zimmerman, Eilene (2001). "What are employees worth?" *Workforce,* 80(2): 32-36.

LINKING TRAINING TO YOUR LIBRARY'S
MISSION AND VISION

Anonymous (1999). "Is your training operation obsolete? Yes if you are not running it like a business." *The New Corporate University Review,* 7(5): 12-14.

Anonymous (1999). "Strategy-focused groups at all levels are embracing the balanced scorecard." *The New Corporate University Review,* 7(6): 16-17.

Anonymous (2000). "Opening doors." *Human Resource Executive,* 14(12): A1-A34.

Anonymous (2000). "Using strategy maps to align training with business goals." *Corporate University Review,* 8(6): 1, 10-11.

Anonymous (2001). "How to measure the 'soft' business results of your training programs." *National Productivity Review,* 19(4): 27-33.

Brown, Dennis (2001). "Business training becomes strategic." *E-Learning,* 2(1): 21-25.

Caudron, Shari (1998). "Integrate HR and training." *Workforce,* 77(5): 88-93.

Caudron, Shari (2000). "Learning revives training." *Workforce,* 79(1): 34-37.

Clark, Kathryn F. (1999). "Training makeover." *Human Resource Executive,* 13(7): 62-65.

Davenport, Teresa (2001). "Marketing training programs" [Booklet]. Alexandria, VA: ASTD.

Delahoussaye, Martin (2002). "Licking the leadership crisis." *Training,* 39(1): 24-29.

Ellis, Kristine and Gale, Sarah Fister (2001). "Training's seat in the boardroom: A seat at the table." *Training,* 38(3): 90-96.

Jossi, Frank (1999). "Vision makers." *Human Resource Executive,* 13(11): 1, 24-26.

Krell, Eric (2001). "Training earns its keep." *Training,* 38(4): 68-74.

Levant, Jessica (1998). *HRD survival skills: Essential strategies to promote training and development within your organization.* Houston, TX: Gulf Publishing.

Ross, David (1998). "Northern exposure." *People Management,* 4(4): 44-46.

Shank, Patti (1998). "No R-E-S-P-E-C-T? Five foolish things trainers do." *Training & Development,* 52(8): 14-15.

Spitzer, Dean and Conway, Malcolm (2002). "Link training to your bottom line" [Booklet]. Alexandria, VA: ASTD.

van Adelsberg, David and Trolley, Edward A. (1999). "Running training like a business." *Training & Development,* 53(10): 56-65.

Watson, Scott C. (1998). "Five easy pieces to performance measurement." *Training & Development,* 52(5): 44-48.

STARTING A TRAINING PROGRAM

Allerton, Haidee (1996). "What things cost." *Training & Development,* 50(6): 20-23.

Aloian, Dena C. and Fowler, William R. (1994). "How to create a high-performance training plan." *Training & Development,* 48(11): 43-44.

Anonymous (1995). "3 steps for launching a training program without a budget." *Training Directors' Forum Newsletter,* 11(11): 5.

Anonymous (1996). "10 ways to stretch your budget, but keep training quality high." *Training Directors' Forum Newsletter,* 12(1): 7.

Anonymous (2001). "Ten ways to win management support for training programs." *IOMA'S Report on Managing Training & Development,* 1(8): 1, 11-13.

Barron, Tom (1996). "A new wave in training funding." *Training & Development,* 50(8): 28-33.

Boehle, Sarah (2001). "Wired for profit." *Online Learning,* 5(4): 30-36.

Callahan, Madelyn R. (1995). "Training on a shoestring." *Training & Development,* 49(12): 18-23.

Chapnick, Samantha (2000). "Needs assessment for e-learning" [Booklet]. Alexandria,VA: ASTD.

Conway, Mal and Cassidy, Michael F. (2001). "Evaluating trainer effectiveness" [Booklet]. Alexandria, VA: ASTD.

Davenport, Teresa. (2001). "Marketing training programs" [Booklet]. Alexandria, VA: ASTD.

Ekkebus, Christine (1996). "Starting from scratch: Designing training for new plants and modernizations." *Technical & Skills Training,* 7(8): 14-18.

Filipczak, Bob (1996). "Training on the cheap." *Training,* 33(5): 28-34.

Gingerella, Leonard F. (1995). "Seven ways to sell management on training." *Training & Development,* 49(3): 11-13.

Harp, Candice (1995). "Link training to corporate mission." *HR Magazine,* 40(8): 65-68.

Hartley, Darin E. (2001). *Selling e-learning.* Alexandria, VA: ASTD.

Kiser, Kim (2001). "Th`e road ahead." *Online Learning,* 5(9): 16-30.

Krell, Eric (2001). "Training earns its keep." *Training,* 38(4): 68-74.

Kuhn, Nancy (1998). "Training from scratch." *Training & Development,* 52(10): 44-49.

LaBonte, Thomas J. (2001). *Building a new performance vision.* Alexandria, VA: ASTD.

Levant, Jessica (1998). *HRD survival skills: Essential strategies to promote training and development within your organization.* Houston, TX: Gulf Publishing.

McCain, Donald V. (1999). "Aligning training with business objectives." *HR Focus,* 76(2): S1-S3.

Miner, Nanette (2001). "The one-person training department" [Booklet]. Alexandria, VA: ASTD.

Nilson, Carolyn (1999). *How to start a training program: Training is a strategic business tool in any organization.* Alexandria, VA: ASTD.

Raths, David (2001). "A tough audience." *Online Learning,* 5(6): 38-43.

Rosania, Robert J. (2000). *The credible trainer.* Alexandria, VA: ASTD.

Segall, Linda J. (1995). "Selecting and supporting the technical trainer." *Technical & Skills Training,* 6(1): 16-21.

Simpson, Kevin (1996). "Should you outsource technical training or keep it in-house?" *Training & Development,* 53(10): 56-65.

Stamps, David (1995). "Community colleges go corporate." *Training,* 32(12): 36-43.

Van Buren, Mark E. and Erskine, William (2002). "The 2002 ASTD state of the industry report." Alexandria, VA: ASTD.

Wetzel, Matt (2001). "Stuck in the middle." *Online Learning,* 5(2): 30-34.

ROI

The primary published resource on ROI as it relates to training remains Jack J. Phillips' *Return on Investment in Training and Performance Improvement Programs.* First published in 1997, this work provides easily understood guidelines for the preparation and the value of the ROI report. Hence, the select bibliography begins with that book. All else follows.

Phillips, Jack J. (1997). *Return on investment in training and performance improvement programs.* Woburn, MA: Butterworth-Heinemann.

Docent, Inc. (2002). "Calculating the return on your elearning investment." <http://www.docent.com/elearning/ROI_01.html>.

Johnson, Maryfran (2002). "Demystifying ROI." *Computerworld,* April 22, <http://www.computerworld.com/managementtopics/roi/story/0,10801,7032 3,00.html>.

Kurtus, Ron (n.d.). "Return-on-Investment (ROI) from e-learning, CBT and WBT." <http://www.school-for-champions.com/elearning/roi.htm>.

Kusack, James Michael (2002). "Understanding and Controlling the Costs of Library Services." *Library Administration and Management,* 16(3): 151-155.

Phillips, Jack J. (1996). "Measuring the ROI: The fifth level of evaluation." *Technical and Skills Training,* April, p. 10.

ADDITIONAL SELECTED BIBLIOGRAPHY ON ROI

Davidove, E. A. (1993). "Evaluating the return on investment of training." *Performance and Instruction,* 32(1): 1-8.

Phillips, Jack J. (Ed.) (1994). *In Action: Measuring return on investment, Volume 1.* Alexandria,VA: American Society for Training and Development.

Phillips, Jack J. (1995). "Corporate training: Does it pay off?" *William and Mary Business Review,* summer, pp. 6-10.

Phillips, Jack J. (1996). "How much is the training worth?" *Training & Development,* April, pp. 20-24.

Phillips, Jack J. (1996). "ROI: The search for best practices." *Training & Development,* February, pp. 42-47.

Phillips, Jack J. (1996). "Was it the training?" *Training & Development,* March, pp. 28-32.

Phillips, Jack J. (Ed.). (1997). *In Action: Measuring Return on Investment, Volume 2.* Alexandria, VA: American Society for Training and Development.

Phillips, Jack J. (1998). "Level four and beyond: An ROI model." In S. M. Brown and C. J. Seidner (Eds.), *Evaluating corporate training* (pp. 113-140). Boston, MA: Kluwer Academic Publishers.

Phillips, Jack J. (2000). *The consultant's scorecard.* New York: McGraw-Hill.

Phillips, Jack J. and Phillips, Patricia Pulliam (1998). *Mastering ROI.* Alexandria, VA: American Society for Training and Development.

Phillips, Jack J. and Phillips, Patricia Pulliam (2000). "The return-on-investment process: Issues and trends." *Training Journal,* October, pp. 8-12.

Phillips, Jack J., Phillips, Patricia Pulliam, and Duresky, Lizette Zuniga (2000). "Evaluating the effectiveness and the return on investment of e-learning." In M. E. Van Buren (Ed.), *What works online*. Alexandria,VA: American Society for Training and Development.

Phillips, Jack J. and Stone, Ron D. (2002). *How to measure training results*. New York: McGraw-Hill.

Phillips, Jack J., Stone, Ron D., and Phillips, Patricia Pulliam (2001). *The human resources scorecard: Measuring the return on investment*. Boston, MA: Butterworth-Heinemann.

Phillips, Patricia Pulliam (Ed.) (2001). *In Action: Measuring return on investment, Volume 3*. Alexandria, VA: American Society for Training and Development.

Phillips, Patricia Pulliam (Ed.) (2002). *In Action: Measuring ROI in the Public Sector*. Alexandria, VA: American Society for Training and Development.

Phillips, Patricia Pulliam and Burkett, Holly (2001). *Managing evaluation shortcuts*. Alexandria, VA: American Society for Training and Development.

RECRUITMENT AND RETENTION ISSUES

Ainsbury, Bob (2000). "The revenge of the library scientist." *Online* 23(6): 60-62.

ARL (1995). *Non-librarian professionals*. SPEC Kit 212. Washington, DC: Association of Research Libraries.

ARL (1999). *Library support staff position classification studies*. SPEC Kit 252. Washington, DC: Association of Research Libraries.

ARL (2000). *Changing roles of library professionals*. SPEC Kit 256. Washington, DC: Association of Research Libraries.

ARL (2000). *The M.L.S. hiring requirement*. SPEC Kit 257. Washington, DC: Association of Research Libraries.

Berry III, John N. (2000). "Educating for library jobs [editorial]." *Library Journal* 125(17): 6.

Biele, Penny and Adams, Megan M. (2000). "Other duties as assigned: Emerging trends in the academic library job market." *College and Research Libraries* 61(4): 336-347.

Blixrud, Julia (2000). "Bk-Room and Front-Line Changes." *ARL* 208/209: 14-15.

Bosseau, Don L. and Martin, Sue K. (1995). "The accidental profession: Seeking the best and the brightest." *Journal of Academic Librarianship* 21(3): 198-199.

Bridges, William (1994). "The end of the job." *Fortune* 130(6): 62+.

Cappelli, Peter (2001). "Making the most of on-line recruiting." *Harvard Business Review* 79(3): 139-146.

"College librarians remain busy in the age of the Internet" (2001). *Chicago Sun-Times,* January 9, p. 7.

Crosby, Olivia (2001). "Librarians: Information experts in the information age." *Occupational Outlook Quarterly* 44(4): 1-15.

Deiss, Kathryn (2000). "Changing roles in research libraries." *ARL* 208/209: 15.

Dillon, Jon, Skinner, Cindy, Swanson, Mary (1998). "Sharing the wealth: Paraprofessionals at Oregon State University Valley Library." *OLA [Oregon Library Association] Quarterly* 4(Fall): 3.

Greenhouse, Steven (2000). "Proposed raise for librarians dropped after city objects." *The New York Times,* September 17, p. 46.

Gregory, Vickie L. (1999). "Beating inflation now." *Library Journal* 124 (17): 36-42.

Gregory, Vickie L. and McCook, Kathleen d.I.P. (1998). "Breaking the $30K barrier." *Library Journal* 123(17): 32-38.

Gregory, Vickie L. and Wohlmuth, Sonia R. (2000). "Better pay, more jobs." *Library Journal* 125(17): 30-36.

Joinson, Carla (2001). "Refocusing job descriptions." *HR Magazine* 46(1): 66-72.

Kaufman, Paula T. (2002). "Where do the next 'we' come from? Recruiting, retaining, and developing our successors." *ARL Bimonthly Report* 221, April. Available at <http://www.arl.org/newsltr/221/recruit. htm>.

Kyrillidou, Martha (2000). "Educational credentials, professionalism, and librarians" *ARL* 208/209: 12-13.

Kyrillidou, Martha (2000). "Salary trends highlight inequities—Old and new." *ARL* 208/209: 6-12.

Lippincott, Joan (2000). "Librarians and cross-sector teamwork." *ARL* 208/209: 22-23.

Mallory, Maria (2001). "Tech jobs: Librarians breaking out of the bookish mold." *The Atlanta Constitution,* February 28, p. 15D.

Matarazzo, James M. (2000). "Who wants to be a millionaire (sic librarian!)." *Journal of Academic Librarianship* 26(5): 309-310.

"Out in the field: Hiring demand, salaries rise for librarians" (2001). *Boston Globe,* January 12, p. M2.

PLA (2000). "Recruitment of public librarians: A report to the Executive Committee of the Public Library Association." *Public Libraries* 39(3): 168-172.

Quint, Barbara (2000). "Recruiting a corporate dream team [librarians make great additions to information industry organizations]." *Information Today* 17(8): 12-13.

Schneider, Karen G. (2000). "My money, my life: The librarian's image, unrevised." *The New York Times* October 29, p. 11.

St. Lifer, Evan (2000). "The boomer brain drain: The last of a generation?" *Library Journal* 125(8): 38-42.

"Undergrad programs the rage [LJ News]" (2000). *Library Journal* 125 (December): 22.

White, Herbert (1998). "White papers: What is a professional in our field? [editorial]." *Library Journal* 123(3): 117-118.

Wilson, Craig (2001). "Stacks of reasons to be thankful for librarians." *USA Today,* January 17, p. 1D.

Wisner, William H. (2001). "Librarianship enters the twilight [opinion]." *Library Journal* 125 (January) 68.

TRAIN THE TRAINER

Although there are "train-the-trainer" learning resources available in a variety of formats including coaching manuals, video recordings, booklets, and pamphlets, many of these are specific to a particular discipline or industry. Therefore, the following are selected and suggested as applicable to training trainers, in general, and may be of use to those considering this area of training in their library to expand the in-house cadre of staff trainers.

Charles, C. Leslie (1998). *The instant trainer: Quick tips on how to teach others what you know.* New York: McGraw-Hill.

Goad, Tom W. (1997). *The first-time trainer: A step-by-step quick guide for managers, supervisors, and new training professionals.* New York: AMACOM.

Ittner, Penny L. (1997). *Train the trainer.* Amherst, MA: HRD Press.

Jolles, Robert L. (1993). *How to run seminars and workshops: Presentation skills for consultants, trainers, and teachers.* New York: John Wiley and Sons.

Lange, Arthur J., Jakubowski, Patricia, and McGovern, Thomas V. (1976). *Responsible assertive behavior: Cognitive behavioral procedures for trainers.* Champaign, IL: Research Press.

Rae, Leslie (1996). *Lesson plans for teaching basic training skills to new trainers.* New York: McGraw-Hill.

Rosania, Robert J. (2001). *The credible trainer: Create value for training, get respect for your ideas, and boost your career.* Alexandria, VA: ASTD.

Sloman, Martyn (2002). *The e-learning revolution: How technology is driving a new training paradigm.* New York: AMACOM.

Smith, Barry J. (1987). *How to be an effective trainer: Skills for managers and new trainers.* New York: John Wiley and Sons.

Taylor, Kathleen, Marienau, Catherine, and Fiddler, Morris (2000). *Developing adult learners: Strategies for teachers and trainers.* San Francisco: Jossey-Bass.

SELECTED ANNOTATED BIBLIOGRAPHY OF DONALD L. KIRKPATRICK'S PUBLISHED WORKS

Kirkpatrick, Donald L. (1975). *Evaluating training programs.* Alexandria, VA: American Society for Training and Development.

Item Type: Book
ISBN: 9-99525-267-8
Terms: Return-on-Investment (ROI). HRD program evaluation. Instructional evaluation.

A collection of articles from the *Training & Development* Journal.

Kirkpatrick, Donald L. (1982). *How to improve performance through appraisal and coaching.* New York: American Management Association.
Item Type: Book
ISBN: 0-8144-5719-3
Terms: Coaching. Performance appraisals. Performance management.

Part II contains examples from different organizations.

Kirkpatrick, Donald L. (1983). *A practical guide for supervisory training and development,* Second edition. Reading, MA: Addison-Wesley.
Item Type: Book
ISBN: 0-201-13435-7
Terms: Supervisory development.

Contains case studies of effective programs

Kirkpatrick, Donald L. (1985). *How to manage change effectively: Approaches, methods, and case examples.* San Francisco, CA: Jossey-Bass.
Item Type: Book
ISBN: 0-87589-659-6
Terms: Change management.

Kirkpatrick, Donald L. (1987). *How to plan and conduct productive business meetings.* New York: American Management Association.
Item Type: Book
ISBN: 0-8144-7664-3
Terms: Meeting management. Kirkpatrick, Donald L. Guidelines.

Written for those responsible for planning and running and meetings. Provides practical suggestions for those that conduct meetings in industry, business, government, the military, schools, churches, volunteer organizations, and other types of organizations. Sections discuss when meetings are necessary, what makes meetings productive, cost of nonproductive meetings, causes of nonproductive meetings and solutions, role of the leader, how to prepare for meetings, how to present information effectively, how to get and maintain enthusiastic involvement, how to control a meeting, how to conclude a meeting, how to coordinate a meeting, how to evaluate meetings and improve future meetings, how to conduct brainstorming meetings, and how to conduct problem-solving meetings. Also contains tips on how to conduct in-house instructional meetings, how to conduct sales meetings, how to use teleconferences, and how to contribute as a participant. Appendixes contain Murphy's Law at meetings, audiovisual aids, practical tips from trained and experienced meeting leaders, and guidelines for leading group meetings.

Kirkpatrick, Donald L. (Ed.) (1987). *More evaluating training programs.* Alexandria, VA: American Society for Training and Development.
Item Type: Book
ISBN: 1-56286-028-3
Terms: HRD program evaluation. Instructional evaluation. Evaluation designs. Evaluation instruments.

Reprints all evaluation articles from *Training & Development* journal from 1976-1986.

Kirkpatrick, Donald L. (1993). *How to train and develop supervisors.* New York: American Management Association.
Item Type: Book
ISBN: 0-8144-5148-9
Terms: Supervisory development. Guidelines. Case studies.

Provides a complete and pragmatic guide to creating or improving responsive, timely, and effective supervisory training and development programs. Presents a systematic approach, with explanations of the concepts, procedures, and techniques that will ensure good programs in organizations of all sizes. Supplies eleven case studies that demonstrate how a variety of organizations run their programs on a daily basis, deal with both common and uncommon problems, and develop innovative approaches.

Kirkpatrick, Donald L. (1993). "Riding the winds of change." *Training & Development* 47(2): 29-32.
Item Type: Journal article
Terms: Change management. Guidelines.

Discusses how managers can get the support of their staff during an organization change. Presents a survey that readers can use to assess their own attitudes about implementing change. Lists reasons why people resist change and why they will accept or even welcome change.

Kirkpatrick, Donald L. (1994). *Evaluating training programs: The four levels.* San Francisco, CA: Berrett-Koehler.
Item Type: Book
ISBN: 1-881052-49-4
Terms: Evaluation instruments. Evaluation designs. HRD program evaluation. Kirkpatrick, Donald L. Evaluation models. Many companies. Guidelines. Case studies.

Designed for practitioners in the training field who plan, implement, and evaluate training programs. Presents guidelines, principles, and sample survey forms for each step of the process. Includes thirteen detailed case studies of companies that have evaluated their training programs using one or more of the four levels.

Kirkpatrick, Donald (1996). "Revisiting Kirkpatrick's four-level model." *Training & Development* 50(1): 54-57.
Item Type: Journal article
Terms: HRD program evaluation. Evaluation instruments. Evaluation models. Kirkpatrick, Donald L. HRD gurus. Historical studies. Models. Guidelines.

Contains a condensed version of the original four articles by Donald Kirkpatrick on evaluating training programs that appeared in *Training & Development* in November 1958 to February 1959. Contains commentary from the author thirty-seven years after the original model was published. Discusses modifications that have been made to the original model and presents guidelines for implementation.

Kirkpatrick, Donald L. (1996). "Evaluation." In Craig, Robert L. (Ed.), *The ASTD training and development handbook: A guide to human resource development* (pp. 294-312). New York: McGraw-Hill.
Item Type: Book chapter, handbook
ISBN: 0-07-013359-X
Terms: Evaluation designs. Evaluation instruments. Kirkpatrick, Donald L. Guidelines. Theories. Models.

Chapter 14. Encourages training professionals to take an in-depth look at evaluation. Stresses that evaluation will impact the future of their programs. Clarifies the meaning of evaluation by breaking it into parts: reaction, training, behavior, and results. Includes several sample evaluation instruments.

Kirkpatrick, Donald L. (Ed.) (1998). *Another look at evaluating training programs.* Alexandria, VA: American Society for Training and Development.
Item Type: Book
ISBN: 1-56286-088-7
Terms: Tests. Return-on-Investment (ROI) Evaluation models. Questionnaires. Guidelines. Models.

Consists of a compilation of articles from ASTD publications over the past ten years on the topic of evaluation of training programs. Articles provide an overview of theoretical and philosophical approaches to training evaluation, as well as specific approaches and techniques for evaluating training. A special section, dealing with return on investment issues, is included. Also includes sections on creating tests and employee surveys to collect data.

Index

THE PRACTICAL LIBRARY TRAINER

_____in hardbound at $22.46 (regularly $29.95) (ISBN: 0-7890-2267-2)

_____in softbound at $13.46 (regularly $17.95) (ISBN: 0-7890-2268-0)

Or order online and use special offer code HEC25 in the shopping cart.

COST OF BOOKS_____

OUTSIDE US/CANADA/
MEXICO: ADD 20%_____

POSTAGE & HANDLING_____
(US: $5.00 for first book & $2.00
for each additional book)
(Outside US: $6.00 for first book
& $2.00 for each additional book)

SUBTOTAL_____

IN CANADA: ADD 7% GST_____

STATE TAX_____
(NY, OH, MN, CA, IN, & SD residents,
add appropriate local sales tax)

FINAL TOTAL_____
(If paying in Canadian funds,
convert using the current
exchange rate, UNESCO
coupons welcome)

☐ **BILL ME LATER:** ($5 service charge will be added)
(Bill-me option is good on US/Canada/Mexico orders only;
not good to jobbers, wholesalers, or subscription agencies.)

☐ Check here if billing address is different from
shipping address and attach purchase order and
billing address information.

Signature_____

☐ **PAYMENT ENCLOSED: $**_____

☐ **PLEASE CHARGE TO MY CREDIT CARD.**

☐ Visa ☐ MasterCard ☐ AmEx ☐ Discover
☐ Diner's Club ☐ Eurocard ☐ JCB

Account # _____

Exp. Date_____

Signature_____

Prices in US dollars and subject to change without notice.

NAME_____

INSTITUTION_____

ADDRESS_____

CITY_____

STATE/ZIP_____

COUNTRY_____ COUNTY (NY residents only)_____

TEL_____ FAX_____

E-MAIL_____

May we use your e-mail address for confirmations and other types of information? ☐ Yes ☐ No
We appreciate receiving your e-mail address and fax number. Haworth would like to e-mail or fax special
discount offers to you, as a preferred customer. **We will never share, rent, or exchange your e-mail address
or fax number.** We regard such actions as an invasion of your privacy.

Order From Your Local Bookstore or Directly From
The Haworth Press, Inc.
10 Alice Street, Binghamton, New York 13904-1580 • USA
TELEPHONE: 1-800-HAWORTH (1-800-429-6784) / Outside US/Canada: (607) 722-5857
FAX: 1-800-895-0582 / Outside US/Canada: (607) 771-0012
E-mailto: orders@haworthpress.com
PLEASE PHOTOCOPY THIS FORM FOR YOUR PERSONAL USE.
http://www.HaworthPress.com

BOF03